SIKHISM AND SPIRITUALITY

Life is a great gift from God to mankind, of who is oblivious to this gift. Guru Nanak, the spiritual master of the Sikhs in Punjab, India knew and wrote about it in the Sikh Holy Book, Sri Guru Granth Sahib. The purpose of life, according to Guru Nanak, is to merge with our Creator, God. For that, one has to live a truthful life earning honestly, sharing it with the needy and meditating on God to fall in love with Him and seek His Grace to be one with Him.

According to Guru Nanak, there is one God and we are all equal and His Children. He is the creator and controls the universe with His Will and we all work to this Will. He loves His Universe and us. His saints, who are in love with Him and with His Grace, are merged with Him. They spread His message of truth to other people around them.

Maya, another invisible creation of God, is keeping us away from Him by creating a wall of doubts and ideas of duality about Him in our mind. This gets His play going in this universe. Once we overcome these doubts by meditating on God, our mind (a child of God) becomes clean and pure and becomes one with God- The True Being. This gives our mind spirituality. Then for that mind there are no anxieties and worries; all is bliss and peace. This book deals with God's world in which we are born and explains methods to make our minds pure by controlling our thoughts, speech and karmas to be pure. This leads us to a path of spirituality; bliss and peace forever and freedom from rebirths on earth.

SIKHISM AND SPIRITUALITY

Rabinder Singh Bhamra

Library of Congress Control Number:		2015908582
ISBN:	Hardcover	978-1-5035-7238-6
	Softcover	978-1-5035-7240-9
	eBook	978-1-5035-7239-3

To order additional copies of this book, contact:
Xlibris
1-888-795-4274
www.Xlibris.com
Orders@Xlibris.com
705449

CONTENTS

DEDICATED

TO ALL SEEKING UNITY WITH THEIR SPIRITUAL FATHER
AND MOTHER RESIDING INSIDE THEIR BODY AND WHOLE
UNIVERSE AND PRAYING FOR HIS BLESSINGS TO ACCEPT
THEM IN HIS TRUE HOME AND LIVE IN PEACE AND BLISS

PREFACE

This book is a collection of essays written on topics on Sikhism and Spirituality which I wrote on a Sikh forum during Gurmat discussions between a period of 2003 and 2011. The purpose was to let people know about Gurmat which I had learnt during 1973 till now during my volunteer service in the Gurdwara at Richmond Hill in New York City, as a Secretary, Trustee and Vice President for 19 years. The sewa included doing kirtan, service to Sangat, learning about the Sikh religion, Gurbani, classical music and Naam Japna in the company of Sadh Sangat. I gained a lot from the Guru Granth Sahib, the Sikh holy book and holy congregation which changed my life and thinking. I got all my answers on life from Guru Granth Sahib who guides man to become spiritual and be one with God. It took me about two months till I was able to silence my mind and go into Sunn (thoughtless mind and body in Smadhi) after I started doing Naam Japna (meditation on God) in the company of Sadh Sangat (Holy Congregation). The progress went on under the guidance of Late Bhai Sahib Sewa Singh Ji from Moga, India. I hope this book will serve as a good guidance to the beginners, ones on the path of spirituality and may motivate some non-believers to become believers. Modern men who have studied science (with no knowledge about religion and spirituality) become mostly gullible and non-believers. They want to see God and the soul before they believe in them. They think they do not exist as they cannot see or measure them.

There is a big change in our education system. It used to be in religious places where religion was compulsory. The students who came out of school were mostly believers. But now education has shifted to public schools where religion is not taught at all and students who come out are mostly non-believers. Science has taken the place of religion. So now, Nature is told to be created by the Big Bang Theory and man is created by the Theory of Evolution- not God. For the modern man religion is science. Everything which is visible or measurable is true and if they cannot see or measure a thing, it is not true. Thus scientists and rationalists miss experiencing things that they cannot see or measure. The mind has to be trained in techniques for meditation so that it gains spiritual power and becomes independent of Maya (thoughts of the visible world) which affects our mind and produces duality- making us attached to lust, desire, attachments, anger, ego, worries and anxieties. So far, the scientists and rationalists are concerned more about physical wealth rather than spiritual wealth.

The human life is a great gift to us from God. This stands on the top of the species God created in this world. God made us forget our last lives and made us slaves to Maya. Maya, God's creation, produces duality in our mind. We think we are here in this world to compete with others and come out better placed, more popular and richer than others, not knowing that every one of us belongs to God and is under His Will. This begins God's drama and He enjoys watching this game we play unknowingly for Him. But still every one of us has a chance to be free of Maya (Raj Gun, Tam Gun and Sat Gun) and unite with our Master, God. For this, we need a Guru (spiritual master) to teach us how to get rid of Maya and be strong enough to fight the temptations of desire and to come out victorious in this world to become one with God. Guru Nanak was sent by God on hearing the pleas of the people of Punjab to save them from the tyrant invaders from the Middle East who attacked them every year, looting and killing many of them. It took Guru Nanak 200 years in nine more bodies to train local people to become Saint Soldiers to fight the invaders and stop their attacks. What he did was make them lose control of Maya on their mind through Naam Simran (meditation on God) and make them fearless fighters.

The purpose of human life as taught by the Guru Granth Sahib is to be free of Maya and wake the mind to its true nature-spirituality. This makes them get salvation, or freedom, from rebirth and causes them to love every one, become fearless fighters and forgive others. People believe in ritualistic religion right now and very few have faith in God because of ignorance. They think this is the only life for them. So their view on life is very myopic. Thus people have invited more sufferings in life by their ritualistic beliefs in religion. Their only objective in life is to make as much money/wealth in their life as possible till the end. After death, when they leave this money behind, their kids fight over it and squander it.

The answer to all these problems is being spiritual – that is gaining independence from Maya. Raj Gun and Tam Gun are there for man to use them but soon man develops a weakness for these desires and temptations they offer. And the mind becomes a slave to them, losing independence and becomes asleep to reality. The remedy for the mind is to wake up and lose control of Raj Gun and Tam Gun on the mind by living truthfully and practice Naam Simran. The mind then wakes up to its original true nature – spirituality.

The main remedy for man to achieve permanent bliss and get rid of troubles is Naam Simran. It is elaborated throughout Guru Granth Sahib as to how a change in the human mind to become free of Maya, brings freedom from grief and brings bliss. This is done by Naam Simran and going into Sunn when Anhad Shabad (God's Word) purifies the mind of Tum Gun and Raj Gun and it merges with God who welcomes His child, the mind, home and offers permanent bliss in Nij Ghar- giving freedom from rebirth. The message of the Guru Granth Sahib is very simple and repeated hundreds of time so that man may pick it up somewhere. It outlines problems in human life and gives answers. To reach God one has to love Him and not the visible world. So man rises above the world and meets Him through Sunn (mind quiet and body in smadhi). The person is then liberated while alive. I pray and hope all of us follow this simple way to reach Him and to be full of bliss.

Anhad Sabad is God's utterance, which started His universe and keeps it under His control and carries Naam in it. Naam is God's spiritual energy in His utterance and is responsible for creation and gives it life to reincarnate to higher specie level (there are 8.4 million specie levels in sea, on earth and in sky) till it reaches human level according to its karma and God's grace. Then there is a chance for man's soul to make a union with its Master, God, from where the life started and ends. The man then lives in bliss and is never born again. In that condition, man's mind is fully awake and is spiritual like God Himself. This is the goal of Human life. God is watching and enjoying His game in this world which runs in His Maya. Lucky ones who remember God meditate on Him may become Gurmukh and liberated while alive. The ones who care not for Naam are born again and again, and suffer reincarnation till they know how to stop this cycle of rebirths. Gurbani tells us about God and His creation and everything we got to do win our goal in life. We are sons and daughters of God and must live with our father in the bliss we are looking for on this earth.

The articles have quotes from Sri Guru Granth Sahib in between the paragraphs with page numbers after that. If the quotes are inserted at the end of a paragraph, it ends with a colon and quotes from SGSS are printed right below the last line in between quotation marks. The quotes are given in Roman Punjabi translation of what is given above. Language is simple to understand. This book is published after the success of my previous book named *God's Universe and Man* which is in English poetry. There was a need and desire to print this book on Sikh Spirituality. Different articles are put together to give the reader knowledge and about the obstacles on the way, though one also needs a spiritual teacher, holy company and to lead a life of truth. I am thankful to my wife Balwinder for a lot of encouragement in getting this book ready. I must thank Dr. Jaskiran Ghuman and Avneet Ghuman for their help in the computer work involved. Thanks are also due to Mohn Singh Rattan, a Sikh scholar, who spared his precious time to write a foreword to this book. Last but not least, my sincere thanks to Guru Ji for giving me the spiritual knowledge and ability to express.

Rabinder S Bhamra
Westbury, NY 11590
(516)334-6696 res
rabinderb@aol.com

FOREWORD

I feel privileged to write a few words about 'Sikhism and Spirituality,' a new book by S. Rabinder Singh Bhamra, of New York, U.S.A. The title of the book suggests its focus is on mystical experiences of spiritual planes of a devout seeker of divine knowledge and metaphysical quests. The Sikh religion as propounded by Sri Guru Nanak Dev Ji and as portrayed in the Shabad Guru, Sri Guru Granth Sahib Ji, is a marvelous and monumental discourse on spirituality in the whole range of spiritual philosophies which mankind has known from the ages.

S. Bhamra is a well-known figure, not only in the Sikh community of New York, but in the entire United States of America. A graduate of Khalsa College, Amritsar, he is an engineer by profession. He came to the States about four decades ago and was a successful professional here. It goes to his credit that he brought an intense desire to disseminate the message of Guru Nanak in this part of the world along with his professional activity. He was among the original volunteers of the Sikh Cultural Society of New York, Richmond Hill, the prime institution of the Sikhs. He was among the office bearers of the society and served the community with love and devotion. He performed kirtan of Gurbani and participated in several programs of Naam Simran there and elsewhere.

He is a committed Gursikh and imbibes the spirit of Gur-Shabad in his life. He played a prominent role in the establishment of Jus Punjabi, the first Punjabi TV Station in NY. He had a great passion for using this platform for spreading the message of spiritual excellence of the Sri Guru Granth Sahib. He earned great admiration and acclaim from not only the Sikhs but others who also wanted to know about Sikhism. S. Bhamra is a poet. He has already published a collection of poems in English. His poems, in the backdrop of spirituality of Sri Guru Granth Sahib, have intensity of expression and conviction.

Now, he has come forward with another commendable effort in the shape of this new publication. While going through the pages of this book, I have had the feeling of taking dips in the ocean of peace, tranquility and serenity. It was an amazing experience of my life.

There have been numerous attempts by scholars and academicians to write commentaries on the various aspects of 'Dhur Ki Bani,' but I strongly believe that such works can only be inspiring if one tries to meditate and practice in the realm of Naam Simran and then share the experiences with others.
Sri Guru Granth Sahib is a vast, unfathomable ocean of knowledge. It provides us with guidance on all the issues confronted by humans on this planet, but there is no denying the fact that the base of this knowledge is spiritual in totality. This spirituality leads the seekers to the heights of bliss and union with the Divine.

I am convinced that S. Bhamra has written on this spirituality with the help of his personal devotion and sojourn in the indescribable meandering passages of the unknown world of bliss.

His 53 articles in this book encompass almost every corner of the spirituality of Sri Guru Granth Sahib Ji. Starting with the advent of Guru Nanak Dev Ji in this world to deliver his divine message, the author goes on to explain the deep layers of this message. I have read his articles on SUNN, HUKAM, REINCARNATION, MIRACLES and PANCH SHABAD with great interest and intensity of feeling and I am all praise for the author. He has rightly based everything on NAAM, SURAT and the glory of Naam Simran.

Let me quote a few passages from these articles which have impressed me immensely.

1. God gave Guru Nanak the treasure of Naam to share with others and never asked account for it . . . Guru Ji kept distributing this invaluable gift to his lucky Sikhs. [SatGuru Nanak].
2. What really keeps all the celestial creations in space in place without any support? Gurbani explains that it is held in place by the very Sabad or celestial sound which created these. [Creation of the universe].
3. Anhad means continuous or non-stop. Sabad in Gurbani means the utterance of God . . . This Sabad can be heard by taking our consciousness inside where it resides. [Anhad Sabad]
4. Naam is the divine consciousness, wisdom, intelligence, creative power, plan, will (hukam), light (jot) . . . It is everything that God is. [Naam]

It is extremely difficult to explain the various aspects of spirituality without having a personal experience and passion. S. Bhamra has done it with strong conviction and belief in the grace of the Guru. His exposition of Laavaan, a composition of our fourth Guru Sahib has really inspired me.

All these articles have already been the focus of various learning forums on the internet and elsewhere and I feel the true seekers have gained a sublime feeling of spirituality in these exercises.

I welcome the publication of all these articles in the book form. I congratulate the author on his hard work and recommend the readers, especially those interested in spirituality, to enjoy.

Mohan Singh Rattan, M.A., Ph.D.
Tampa, Florida, U.S.A.
March 14, 2015.

Dr. Mohan Singh Rattan, a prolific writer and academician, started his career as a Journalist. He was on the editorial board of Punjabi dailies; Ajit, Akali Patrika, Jathedar and Qaumi Dard. He has master's degrees in Punjabi and English from Punjab University, Chandigarh and Guru Nanak Dev University, Amritsar, respectively. He obtained his Ph.D from Punjab University, Chandigarh in 1977. The topic of his thesis was: Concept of Bliss in Sri Guru Granth Sahib. His research work on 'Sidh Gosat' a composition of Sri Guru Nanak Dev Ji has been well received by the academic world. He was Lecturer in Punjabi at Lyall Pur Khalsa College, Jalandhar and Sikh National Collage Charan Kanwal, Banga for six years.

He worked for 28 years in Punjab University Text Book Board as an Academician and Editor of books in medium switchover program in Punjabi. Presently, he is, guiding the Sikh Heritage College, Tampa FL USA as founder Principal.

INTRODUCTION

Sikhism is a world religion which was declared in Punjab, India with the advent of Guru Nanak, who was born near Lahore in 1469 AD. Guru Nanak was a divine teacher and started preaching to the people in 1499 AD after he had a revelation from God to preach his divine message. He believed in One God, who is the God of all live beings in the world. God is responsible for all the creation in the universe, which is infinite, and controls it by His Will. We are all His children and equal. He lives within His creation as a soul, a part of Himself. He is both immanent and transcendent; thus He lives within His universe and outside the whole infinite universe of His. He is beyond death and is not born, neither. He is self-existent. He has been the same all the time. We can see and meet Him with His Grace. He loves His universe and takes care of it whether in sea, or on land and in air. There are 8.4 million species in the world and man stands on top of this list.

All live beings have a mind and this mind is used to think in addition to the presence of their soul, which gives them life. Mind is a child of God and lives with its body. It has consciousness, intelligence and wisdom according to what is granted to that mind by God to each one as per his/her destiny. The Mind uses consciousness to observe and then decides to take action according to its wisdom and intelligence. Consciousness thus tells the brain to create a physical action with its body. This action by the body is called *Karma*. There is an accumulation of karmas by the body during its life time. The thinking process of the mind is controlled by another factor called

Maya. Maya is another creation of God and thrown into His Universe. The job of Maya is to make you forget God, produce duality and doubts to become attached to His physical Universe. Maya has three qualities: Rajas Mode, Tamas Mode and Satvic Mode. Rajas mode creates hopes, ambitions, anxieties etc. Tamas Mode creates lust, anger, greed, attachments, ego, hatred, slandering etc. Satvic mode creates kindness, contentment, discipline, charity, meditation etc. One has to avoid Rajas Mode and Tamas Mode and, basically, live in Satvic Mode to live clean. But to live pure one has to accumulate the power of Naam in the mind till it is pure as God and merge with Him in order to attain spirituality.

However, the Mind has to be purified by Naam through Naam Japna (meditating on God). Naam is the power of God within you and one has to get rid of unnecessary thoughts from the mind. The Mind does not stop thinking about the world all the time. By doing Naam Japna, one can control these thoughts. This unstopped thinking process in the mind is called to be living in *Bhavjal Sagar* or Terrifying World Ocean. One has to still the mind to make it thoughtless. This is done by Naam Japna which is meditation on gur-mantra –Waheguru. This is fully explained in the chapter on Naam Japna. After continuous chanting regularly day after day the mind goes into sunn, or quiet mode, and the body goes into in Smadhi Mode. One can hear Anhad Sabad (nonstop musical sounds heard within the ears but not audible to the outside world) in conscious mode and later in Sunn Mode. Further progress can lead to hearing sehaj-dhun-a sharp low volume whistle. That is where angels live. One is then just outside the tenth door, or gateway, to enter God's House. If God is pleased, He opens the door to the True House and lets the seeker in where he/she is greeted with Panch-Sabad (five musical notes) and then greeted by God. The mind then reaches the house from where the whole journey on land started. He is welcome back by God, where he enjoys peace and bliss. The Mind thus reaches Nij-Ghar, or its own house. The mind can come back to the body on Earth for the rest of its destined life but has the privilege to go back to Nij- Ghar whenever it chooses. After death, the mind is then is freed from any reincarnation and is allowed to stay in Nij-Ghar till Father gives him/her any assignment in His Universe.

The life of the human body is counted by the number of days and the number of breaths it is allowed on earth. The mental/sookham body is taken to God in order to write the judgment, or the destiny, of the person for the next life. The mental body lives in the air till its next parents are found. The person is then born again and lives a life of happiness and or grief. This can go on till the person's mind is pure to meet God. There is no heaven or hell in the Sikh religion. Heaven is ending life with God, and Hell is getting born again and again-which is a punishment in and of itself. This is very well explained in the four articles titled 'Death and After' towards the end of this book. Reincarnation into different specie levels is a must for those who do not remember God during their life time. They are called Man-Mukhs. Those who meet God during their life time are called Gur-Mukhs as they are not reincarnated and enjoy peace and bliss in the heavenly house.

The above knowledge is given by Guru Nanak and later on by nine more Sikh Gurus. The tenth Guru, Guru Gobind Singh, compiled the Gurbani of earlier Gurus and the thirty five saints of other religions into a Holy Book called Guru Granth Sahib and declared it to be the last Guru, thus ending the line of Gurus in human form. The Guru Granth Sahib has all the spiritual knowledge of the Gurus and saints who were one with God. It tells about God, His universe and life on Earth. It tells how to avoid unhappiness and how to live in peace and happiness on Earth. It fully explains God's Will and tells the human being that the aim of human life is to be one with God by living a pure life and meditating on God. Becoming One with God, man reaches their spiritual home, reincarnation stops and man regains peace and bliss forever which he or she is seeking on earth. The man finds out that life on Earth was just a dream and that they were just playing a game during life for God when the five 'doots' (evil spirits) of Maya had complete control of the Mind.

Gurbani contained in the Guru Granth Sahib is called 'Dhur Ki Bani'. It is the word of God which came through our Gurus, who were one with God, and they translated it into our own language for us to read, understand and act upon. Gurbani further tells us that God lives within us and we need not go into jungles or elsewhere to seek Him. One should lead a married life, earn an honest living, join in the holy congregation and meditate on God for making us free from attachments, desires and temptations. So we must wake our mind to the reality that we are God's children who were sent to earth to play a game for Him. Sants, sadhus, bahgats and brahmgianis are saints that are one with God and their job on earth is to teach us the true path leading to union with God. They are our spiritual teachers and demand our respect and service. They do not make any physical demands on us as it is their duty to serve us. But be careful of false saints who advertise their tour and charge compensation for anything they do for us.

Khalsa is a saint-soldier who was created by Guru Gobind Singh Ji. Guru Ji told the people that Khalsa is the Army Of God and Khalsa came into being to the pleasure of God. Khalsa's job was to fight for truth and justice for the common man. Khalsa drove the Middle-Eastern invaders away to their homes and the advent of Guru Nanak was honored by God for this help. There are still some Khalsas residing in Punjab who live by the old customs. Their favorite ride is on the horse, fully armed the old way and they are ready to fight for truth and justice at a moment's notice.

Towards the end of the book there are some chapters on 'Understanding Gurbani'. Gurbani is written in Gurmukhi script. The language used carries within itself the spiritual knowledge expressed in our language, which is sometimes difficult for spiritual expression. To understand it one has to be on a spiritual plane. Some examples are given to clarify the meaning of some words and sentences. That is why Gurbani could mean different things to different people.

In the end, I would like to say something regarding spirituality, again. According to Sikhism, it is the state of mind in which being with the mind's true self that the spirit is within us: the atma/the soul/ God and behaves like the One all the time. One may experience this oneness while spiritually elevated at different occasions, but unless it is a permanent change in the mind, it may be close to spirituality but not true spirituality. In the end of the book I wrote about Laavan, or marriage hymns, written by Guru Ji. It is about the spiritual marriage of the Spirit/Soul with God. It tells how the pure mind/soul purifies itself through four stages and becomes one with God. The Soul ultimately meets the Husband Lord, lives happy and in bliss ever afterwards.

The reader may say there is no continuity in this book. Various chapters are just thrown together but not related to each other. But one must realize who started this religion, when it started and if there is any documentation for the Sikh religion. Guru Nanak Dev Ji started this religion in 1499 AD. He wrote his Gurbani in a Pothi. The fifth Guru, Arjan Dev Ji, compiled the first Pothi, or Holy Book of Gubani, containing the Gurbani of his own, the earlier four Gurus and thirty five saints. Later on Guru Gobind Singh Ji compiled the Guru Granth Sahib adding the Gurbani of His father, Guru Teg Bahadur Ji. The originals are still there. Khalsa fought with the invaders to make Punjab free and ruled over it for fifty years. So now, we have the Guru Granth Sahib amidst us and guiding us as a Guru. The chapters later on tell us what Sikhs believe regarding God, God's Hukam, Consciousness, Mind, Naaam, Nij Ghar, Sunn, Astral Body, Sikhs and their Religon, Khalsa etc. Various steps leading to understanding the principles of the Sikh religion and spirituality are fully explained in various chapters for the seeker to understand. Chapters toward the end of the book explain death in detail.

I must thank many a saintly spirit I had met in America and gained so much spiritual knowledge from them. The Gurbani of Guru Granth Sahib, Keertan and Holy Congregation was the source of my inspiration in the Sikh Way of life on this planet. Guru Ji guided my entire life here and came to help me in writing of this book.

SATGURU NANAK

It was in the year 1469 AD that Guru Nanak, a divine being, took birth at Talwandi near Lahore. Guru Nanak was a messenger of God whom He had sent down as a Satguru, a True and Divine Teacher. Under the Satguru's guidance one can get liberation from the cycle of births and deaths and become one with the Creator God by meditating on God's Name and singing His praises:

"Sat Purakh jin jaania Satgur tis ka naaon.
Tiske sang sikh ubre Nanak Har gun gaaon." p-286

Although born with a mission, yet Guru Nank did not start delivering the message till 1499 AD after he had a revelation, an encounter with God. Guru Nanak went for a bath at the River Beini and disappeared under the water and reappeared after three days. Janam Sakhi states this event: 'As God willed, Nanak was escorted to His Divine Presence and a cup filled with Amrit was given to him accompanied by the command', 'Nanak, pay attention! This is the cup of Holy Adoration of My Naam, drink it. I am with thee and thee do I bless and exalt. Go rejoice in My Naam and preach to others to do the same. Let this be thy calling.' Guru Nanak Ji himself comments on this event in his Gurbani, 'An insignificant bard at the Gate of Lord was I. My assignment was to sing His praises day and night. True Lord now has called me to His Mansion and there I go robed in Honor of His Divine Naam':

"Hau dhaadee vekaar kare laayaa.
Raat dihe ke kaar dhurau furmaayaa.
Dhaadee sachay mehal Khasam bulaaiaa.
Sachee sifat slaah kapraa paaiaa." p-150

God delivered the food of ambrosial nectar of Naam. Those, following Guru's advice partook in it and dwelled in peace and happiness. I, His minstrel sing His glories and enjoy this spiritual food of Naam He gave me. Thus praising the True One I have become one with Him':

"Sachaa Amrit Naam bhojan aaiaa.
Gurmatee khaadhaa ruj tin sukh paaiaa.
Dhadee kare pasaao Sabad sunaaiaa.
Nanak Sach salaah Pooraa paaiaa." p-150

God gave Guru Nanak, the treasure of Naam to share with others and never asked account for it: "Bhagat bhandaar Guru Nanak kau saunpay. Phir lekhaa mool naa laiaa." p-612. One drop of this nectar of Naam can give liberation to one who takes it and makes him immortal: "Ek boond Gur Amrit deeno taa atal amar na mooaa." p-612. Guru Ji kept distributing this invaluable gift to his lucky Sikhs:

"Satgur Sikh ko Naam dhan deh.
Gur kaa Sikh vadbhaagee heh." p-286

Guru Nanak Dev was commissioned by God to spread His message by singing His glories and sharing the wealth of Naam with humanity as a Satguru, installed by God Himself, the mission for which he spent the rest of his life. For twenty two years starting in 1499 AD Guru Ji traveled on foot almost twenty two thousands miles in all four directions. In each journey, he met the religious leaders of Hindus, Muslims, Sidhas and Yogis from the Sumer Mountains in the Himalayas to Ceylon, from South China and Assam to Mecca and Turkey. He delivered the message by singing with his companion Mardaanaa, a Muslim musician who played Rebab. All these messages were recorded by Guru Nanak in a book he carried with him. Finally Guru Ji settled at Kartaarpur as a farmer. In 1839 he had a dialogue with Sidhas at Batala which is recorded in Gurbani as Sidh Gosht. In Sidh Gosht, Guru Ji describes: the Supreme Being, His creation, the practical way to meet Him through Sunn (absolutely quiet mind), where He resides, and wasteful ways of Jog Matt, which can give supernatural powers but not the illumination of Mind with His Light.

Satguru Nanak came into this world as the savior of Kaljug: "Kal taran Gur Nanak aya" - Bhaee Gurdaas. Guru Nanak brought the Light of spiritual knowledge which destroyed the fog of ignorance: "Satgur Nanak pargatiaa mitti dhund jag chaanan hoaa." - Bhaee Gurdaas. Merciful God did this after listening to the pleas of the people: "Sunee pukaar daattaar Prabh Guru Nanak jug maih paathaayaa."- Bhaee Gurdaas. With continuous attacks by invaders from the Middle East and then the Mughals, the people of Punjab were completely demoralized and the Khatris could not fight to defend the people any more. The first thing Guru Nanak did was to abolish the caste system and declared all human beings to be equal. 'Let it be the responsibility of all to share the burden of defense of the country and not just Khatris, a small percentage of people'. It was an uphill task but he had the assignment to do it with support from Akal Purakh. He made all people sit together, eat together, pray together to One God and prohibited the worship idols of deities. This brought the people together when they needed help most. To make them fearless, he made them meditate on The Fearless: "Nirbhau japay sagal bhau mittay" p-293. He challenged the people's beliefs that life without honor was not worth eating any food: "Jay jeevay patt lathee jaa-ay sabh haraam jetta kich khaa-ay" p-142, and Guru Nanak also complained to God as to how could He not have any mercy on people who were being tyrannized and crying for help:

"Eti maar paee kurlaane
Tain kee dard naa aaiaa." p-360

Guru Nanak's mission continued under nine succeeding Gurus in whom spiritual enlightenment was given at the same level and thus responsibility was transferred by each preceding Guru to the next: "Jot ohaa jugat saaiaa seh kaayaan pher platteeay" p-966. It took almost two hundred years before a cowardly nation of Punjab was transformed into Khalsa, the Saint Soldiers, the army of God, created by God's own plan by the tenth Nanak, Guru Gobind Singh Ji: "Khalsa Akaal Purakh ki fauj. Pargattio Khalsa Parmaatam kee mauj." Khalsa fought fearlessly to free the nation from foreign yoke. They were given the name of Lion and they proved worthy of that name. This completed the mission of Guru Nanak in the tenth form and the people who were meek like lambs, now became lions and were able not only to fight the tyrants but also to defend and support others from them.

The last Guru, Guru Gobind Singh passed the authority of Guruship to the Granth Sahib. Also, the Panj Piaaray were appointed to speak and act for the Granth Sahib in its presence. The Guru Granth Sahib contained the Gurbani of the Gurus and other Indian saints and thus created an everlasting Guru for the Sikhs. "Banee Guru Guru hai banee which banee amrit saaray. Gurbanee kahe sevak jun maanay partakh Guru nistaaray." p-982. Thus the Guru Granth Sahib holds the wisdom of the Guru and guides us as the Guru, and if the disciple follows the instructions of the Gurbani, he will sure meet the Satguru. The need of a Satguru or a Guru in a human form was abolished. So now the Sikhs have the Guru with them forever. Those who want to see the Guru should read and ponder upon Gurbani and then follow the instructions given there repeatedly. If Sikhs have difficulty in understanding Gurbani there are gurmakhs in the Sadh Sangat who have become one with the Guru: "Gursikhan andar Satgur vartay" p-316. They can help and guide others on the spiritual journey. There are also translations available to help.

Guru Nanak simplified the practice of religion to three very simple tenets: Naam Japna (meditation on the Name of God), Kirat Karni (earning one's livelihood honestly) and Wand Shakna (sharing one's earnings and gifts from God with others). One has to live the life of a householder and supporting a family. Bhagti or devotion to God can be done best when one lives in a family. It is not necessary to give up the world to achieve union with God: "Satgur mairay ki wadaee puttar klittar vichay gatt paee" p-661. One has to live a truthful life which means: truthful in thoughts, words and deeds. One needs to develop these qualities to prepare for bhagti: "Vin gun keetay bhagat na hoay" p-4. To achieve union with God one has to connect with Naam which lies inside the body: "Nau nidh Amrit Prabh ka Naam dehi meh is kaa bisraam" p-293. The consciousness of the mind has to go inside the body. That is where Naam Japna comes into play. Repeated recitation of Gurmantra quiets the mind and the mind comes inside where it is cleansed by Naam. When it becomes 'nirmal' or pure, it is ready to meet with Akal Purakh with His Grace. Once His Grace falls on the one seeking Him, one obtains freedom from the shackles of Maya and this leads to permanent bliss. Nothing ever bothers this individual as he realizes His Hukam and his ego merges with Him. He becomes pure, Khalsa, and comes to know that he is the Jot Saroop and becomes like Him:

"Jaisa saivay taisa hoay." p-223

Satguru Nanak showed us the path to freedom then and is showing us even now in Gurbani. We got freedom by following him. But now we have turned away from him and fallen to our own intellect, which is very limited and deals only with the three Gunas of Maya. We are back into the slavery of Maya. We have lost our faith in Satguru and Khande Dee Pauhal. There is no one who will help us but ourselves. We must follow the one who originally made us lions when the people of India looked to the Sikhs for help. So let us sit down and ponder upon our problems and do what our forefathers did: listen to the Guru and follow him as we did many years ago to win our honor and dignity back. Guru Ji is there and speaking to us every time we take a Hukamnama. So let us follow him with full faith and stay in 'chardi kala.'

GURU GRANTH SAHIB, THE ETERNAL GURU

Guru Granth Sahib Ji is our Eternal Guru holding the message of our Eternal Father, Waheguru/Akal Purakh/Parmaatmaa. It was delivered to us by Guru Nanak in ten human forms. Understanding and acting on his message leads to a connection with Naam within us which makes our mind clean and pure. This makes our mind acceptable to our Divine Home with our Father/Mother/ Waheguru/ Parmaatmaa. We then become jiwan-mukat and gain bliss/anand, what we all are looking for in this world. This Holy Scripture of the Sikhs also contains the Bani of six Sikh Gurus and Bahgats, both Hindus and Muslims and makes it the Scripture for humanity in the modern age. Written in Gurmukhi script in Punjabi and Sant Bhasha, which also contains hymns written in Persian, Sanskrit, and other languages of India where the Bhagats belonged to. The Divine Message is expressed in exquisite poetry and set to Raagaas to sing in holy congregation as worship of the Akal Purakh.

Guru Granth Sahib is an ocean of spiritual knowledge and a scripture par excellence for seeker of Truth. One has to dive deep into it to find pearls of Divine Knowledge to guide us on the path to peace and happiness. It is not only a scripture of divine knowledge for humanity but had been given Guruship by Guru Gobind Singh Ji in 1708 at Nander Maharashtra before he left us for his divine home. In the congregation Guru Gobind Singh bowed before Guru Granth Sahib as the next and eternal Guru to lead the Sikhs and Khalsa Panth. So we have to treat it as the Living Guru and give it the same respect whether we are in its presence, transporting it, or when it presides in the congregation. It has to be treated as royalty with truly felt and expressed respect and love from our heart. The scripture has to be treated as the body of the Satguru and bedecked as royalty:

"Guru Granth Ji maanio pargat Guran kee deh." - Panth Parkash

The Satguru is the true friend and the Supreme King, the king of the kings. Sitting in its presence we are exalted and beautified. He is the support of us all:

"Sajan Sachaa Patshaa sir sahaan dai shaah.
Jis paas baithiaan soheeay sabhnaan da vesaah." p-1426

The tradition from the times of Guru Arjun Dev Ji has been the same and the then called Pothi (book containing the holy verses) was laid open under a canopy bedecked with royal robes and an attendant sitting/standing behind with 'chaur', as was done in a king's court as the congregation sat on the floor below. Even Guru Arjun Dev Ji gave the same respect to the Guru Granth Sahib even though it was not declared as a Guru then. But he did declare that this holy book is the seat of God:

"Pothee Parmesar ka thaan." p-1226

Right place for housing the Guru is supposed to be royal and we try to build beautiful Gurdwaras for the same reason. It is for our Spiritual King where we go to see Him, hear Him in keertan and hukamnaama, get His message explained in katha, treated as His children and are fed in His house, and blessed with sanctified 'parsad'. We also pray to Him for His blessings for temporal and spiritual guidance to lead us to live a successful life of happiness. The True Guru is forever merciful to all but without good destiny what can anyone obtain? The True Guru looks at all with same grace beaming from his eyes but we get the rewards according to our love for the Lord:

"Satgur sada dyal hai bhaee vin bhagaan kiaa paeeay.
Ek nadar kar vekhay sabh oopar jehaa bhaao tehaa phal paaeeay."
p-602

Guru Granth Sahib to the Sikhs is the living spirit of the Gurus in Gurbani through which it speaks to them. The Five Piaras in its presence speak to us on His behalf. The Gurbani contained in Guru Granth Sahib is the Guru and carries within it all the nectars we seek. We may feel the spirit of the Guru in its presence and not see it. But once we follow the instructions given in Gurbani for us and live life strictly according to these, we are assured that we can see the Spirit of The True Guru:

"Banee Guru Guru hai banee vich banee amrit saaray.
Gurbani khay sevak jun maanay partakh Guru nistaaray." p-982

Once one sees and enshrines the Guru in one's heart, one gets the bliss one is seeking and says it with pride to the mother, 'This union took place with intuitive ease and my mind is resounding with music of bliss':

"Anand bhaiaa meri maa-ay Satguru maen paaia.
Satgur taa paaiaa sehaj seti mun vajeeaan vadhaaeeaan." p-917

This nectar of Gurbani, the utterance of the Guru came to us from a Sabad, the divine utterance (going on in the entire universe and in live beings). It came to us when the Gurmukh Gurus uttered it to us and later wrote it for us and compiled it as The Granth, now our Guru:

"Sabday upjay amrit banee Gurmukh aakh sunaavaniaa." p-125

This Sabad is the life within all live beings and it is connecting with Sabad that we can meet our Divine Husband Lord:

"Jeaan andar jeeo Sabad hai jit Sauh milaavaa hoay." p-1250

Guru Nanak Dev Ji calls this Sabad as Guru and our 'surti' (consciousness) listening to the music of this Sabad as the disciple or Sikh:

"Sabad Guru surat dhun chelaa." p-943

This Sabad connects us with Naam which further connects us to our Divine Husband Lord within us, The Jot:

"Sbaday hee Naaon upjay Sabday mail milaaia." p-644

And this Jot (divine light) within us is the extension of the Divine and sits within all of us as Satguru, the Immortal Being who neither was born nor dies:

"Satgur mera sada sada naa aavay na jaa-ay.
Oh abinaasee Purakh hai jo sabh meh rahiaa smaa-ay." p-759

Such is the divinely exalted position of Guru Granth Sahib who has been delivered to us from Akal Purakh through the house of Guru Nanak, to help and guide us to seek union with our Creator and receive bliss for which we are looking for in the physical world but fail to get because of our spiritual ignorance and intellectual pride. Thus Guru Granth Sahib came to us as a spiritual ship with its captain to carry us across the sea of maya (world of thoughts), lost in which we suffer, but it emancipates us and unites us with our Creator:

"Guru jhaaj khevat Guru Gur bin tariaa naa koay.
Gur parsaad Prabh paaeeay gurbin mukat na hoay." p-1401

So it becomes of us to go to Guru Ji in utmost humility, love and reverence as if entering the Court of a Supreme King to seek His blessings. We must listen to Him in keertan, katha and accept His Hukamnama as His order for the day to be acted upon in our thoughts, words and deeds.

GOD IN SIKHISM

The fundamental belief in Sikhism is the existence of God, the Creator who is invisible and indescribable but perceivable to anyone who is ready to spend their time and meditation on Him under a spiritual master. In the Holy Book of Sikhism, Guru Granth Sahib, oneness of God is emphasized throughout. God is described in the Mool Mantra, the beginning of the very first page. One God the Creator, His Naam is true, Creator of the Universe, Beyond Fear, Beyond Hatred, Beyond Death, Time, and Self existent, He can be reached by Guru's Grace:

"Ik Onkar Sat Naam Karta Purakh Nirbhau Nirvair Akaal Moorat Ajooni Saibhang Gurparshaad." p-1

The above quote is called Mool Mantra where Mool stands for God. This gives a brief description of God. Sikh Gurus have tried to describe him but the Infinite One is beyond complete description. Nobody knows the power and extent of God. Various seekers of Him and many wise people have tried to do so but have failed to describe Him:

"Har ki gat na koee jaaney.
Jogee jati tapee pach haare aur bauh loag sianey." p-537

God is both in an immanent and transcendent mode which means He lives inside His own created nature and also lives outside of it in the infinite creation as a single changeless, timeless Reality. He is not only contained in His own creation, which He is overseeing and maintaining the way He likes, but pervasive in the entire universe controlling it the way He wants. He uttered one word 'Onkar' which created the total universe. All the play and drama are to Your glory and greatness. The True Lord Himself makes all distinctions; He Himself breaks and builds:

"Onkar sabh srisht upaee.
Sabh khel tamaasha teri vadaee.
Aapay vek kare sabh Saacha Aapey bhun ghraindaa." p-1061

He was true even before time or the beginning of the universe and He was true even after time began. He is true now and Nanak says He will be true in the future:

"Aad Sach jugaad Sach. Hai bhi Sach Nanak hosi bhee Sach." p-1

He is true Himself and whatever He did was true. All creation came into being from the one True God:

"Aap Sach keea sabh Sach. Tis Prabhu tey sagli utpat." p-294

God is transcendent and all pervasive at the same time. Transcendence and immanence are two aspects of the same Supreme Reality. God is in immanent mode for His created world, which as a whole fails to contain Him fully. God Himself is the sole Creator, Sustainer and the Destroyer. Creation is His pleasure and play. He Himself is in transcedent and immanent mode; manifesting His power, He fascinates the entire world:

"Nirgun aap sargun bhee Ohee.
Kaladhaar Jin saglee mohee." p-287

In the void before creation came into being, His first word had the power, or Naam, in it. The whole universe started taking shape.

Whatever happened was because of Naam. There is no place in creation without Naam:

"Jeta keeta teta Naaon. Vin Naavain naheen ko thaaon." p-4

God's Naam is nectar and is equivalent to nine different treasures found in this world. It is also found in the human body:

"Nau nidh Amrit Prabh ka Naam. Dehi mein iskaa bisram." p-293

God is self existent and created Naam out of His Word. Naam created the universe and God relishes sitting within the universe:

"Aapeenay aap saajio aapeene rachio Naaon.
Dooee kudrat saajeeay kar assan ditho chaao." p-463

You are the Creator and everything in this universe is your creation. There is no one other than You:

"Toon Aapay kartaa Teraa keea sabh hoay.
Tudh bin dooja avar naa koay." p-12

God has no fear. This implies sovereignty and unquestioned exercise of His Will. God loves His creation and is the Dispenser of impartial justice. He is the everlasting King afraid of none. No fear can ever come near Him:

"Oh abinaasee raaiaa.
Nirbhau sang Tumaare baste daran khaan te aaiaa." p-206

God is Akaal Moorat or is the Eternal Being. Akaal means beyond time/death and Moorat means form. He is an Infinite Spirit spread over the entire universe and is independent of the universe. Sikhs worship God as Nirankar which means God without form and call Him by that name. So idolatry or image worship is forbidden in any form. You are the Timeless Being and there is no Kaal (time/death) over You. You are not judged and are a unique Inaccessible Being:

"Toon Akaal Purakh naheen sir kaalaa.
Toon Purakh Alekh Agum Niralaa." p-1138

God is Ajuni or Un-incarnated. Primal Creator; God had no creator.
There is no divine-incarnation. God, the Primal Being is beyond
death and birth. By Your Hukam (Order/Will) universe was created;
by creating it You merge in it. Your Form cannot be known. How
can one meditate on You? You are permeating in all and are seen in
Your created Nature:

"Toon Paarbrahm Parmeshar joan na avhee.
Toon Hukmee saje shrisht saaj smavaee.
Tera roop na jaee lakhiaa kion tujhe dhiavaee.
Toon sabh meh varte Aap kudrat dekhvaee." p-1095

God is Saibhang or Self-existent. He cannot be established nor can be
installed by a human being. The Pure One exists by Himself:

"Thaapiaa naa jaa-ay keeta naa hoay.
Aaapay Aap Niranjan Soay." p-2

God can be realized through gur-parsaad. This means God can
be realized through Guru's Grace. Guru, the Ten Sikh Gurus and
Gurbani of Guru Granth Sahib, can be God. The Grace of God is
most essential as nothing is without God's Will or pleasure:

"Hukmay andar sabhko bahir hukam naa koay." p-1

GOD IN SUNN SMADH

God lives in sunn smadh (void/suniya/trance) in His transcendental
mode permeating all of the void. In Gurbani, Satguru (True Guru)
describes that God, The True One, is in sunn smadh in His True
Home:

"Satgur te paa-ay vichaaraa sunn smadh Sachay ghar baaraa." p-1037

In sunn, the Infinite One assumes infinite power. He Himself is Unattached, and Incomprehensible. He Himself creates and beholds His creation from sunn. He produces more sunn. Air and water were created from sunn. He produced the world and body for the mind, which is their ruler:

"Sunn kala aprampar dharee. Aap niraalam apar apaaree.
Aapay kudrat kar kar dekhay sunno sunn upaainda.
Pavan paani sunnay tay saajay. Shrisht uppay kaaiaan garh raajay."
p-1037

The True One lives in Sach Khand within sunn. He keeps on creating more and more in the universe and looks at it with His Graceful eyes. There are planets, planetary systems and galaxies. If one starts describing His creation there is no end to it:

"Sach khand vassay Nirankaar. Kar kar vekhay nadar nihaal.
Tithey khand mandal virbhand. Jay ko kathe taa ant naa ant." p-4

GOD AND MAN

Man is an infinitesimal part of God's creation but it is the only species blessed by God with the ability to reflect, moral sense and the potential to understand metaphysical matters. Being born as a human is a special privilege for a soul as it is conferred a chance for union with God. Of all the 8.4 million species, God bestowed superiority on man:

"Chaurasee lakh joon upaaee.
Manas ko Prabh dee vadiaee." p-1075

God made other species as man's water carriers (servants) and gave man lordship on this Earth:

"Avar joan teri panhaari.
Is dhartee meh teri sikdaaree." p-324

There are four ways He can make His species. The first way is from eggs, the second way is from a placenta, the third way is from sweat and the fourth way is from a seed in earth, growing vegetation everywhere:

"Anadaj jeraj setaj keeni. Utbhuj khaan bauhat rach deeni." - Chaupaee Benanti

Born as a human, the primary objective of man is to seek God within himself. God resides there too. This is the only objective of human life. All other things you do are of no use. The only beneficial thing is to meditate in the company of holy/realized men:

"Bhaee praapat manukh dehuriaa Gobind milan ki eho teri baria. Avar kaaj tere kite na kaam mil sadh sangat bhaj kewal Naam." p-12

The achievement of realization of God rests only in God's grace. Man should believe that God is within him and not far away. He is to seek God in the company of holy men who advise and guide him on the path. He should live a life of a householder, earning by honest means, helping the needy, meditating on God and must wait for His Grace. The result is achievement of peace and bliss when the Grace of God is bestowed on him. The mind then becomes realized or awakened from Maya and achieves spirituality. The mind was manmukh under control of Maya.

GOD AND HIS MAYA

The biggest hurdle on the path of realization is Maya, the intoxicating attraction of man to the visible creation of God. Man, though a spiritual being, is a child of God that falls prey to desires, worries and anxieties created in his mind by Maya. This process takes his mind away from concentration and meditation. God created the world

Himself and made it busy with work. He created the enchantress Maya and put it in the world to work as per His plan to put the whole world astray:

"Tudh Aappe jagat uppaike Aappe dhande laaia.
Moh thagauli paaeyke Tudh Aappe jagat bhlaaia." p-138

The Lord Himself lead us astray in doubts; the Lord Himself gives us understanding:

"Har Aappey bharam bhulaaida Har Appey He matt deh" p-82

Maya is what makes you forget God, produces attachments to the world and creates duality in the mind:

"Eh maya jit Har visre moh upje bhaao duja laaiaa." p-921

Maya influences mind in three modes: 1. Rajas Mode: creates hopes, ambitions, anxieties, worries, etc. 2. Satvic Mode: creates kindness, contentment, sense of duty, discipline, charity, meditation, etc. 3. Tamsic Mode: creates lust, anger, greed, attachments, ego, hatred, slandering, etc. Maya is the biggest obstacle to the mind and it creates non-stop thoughts in the mind which can be stopped only by meditating on God in the company of the holy. One who can kill the thoughts gets salvation (meets God), helps others and is never born again:

"Veechaar maarey turray taarrey ult joan na aavay." p-687

MORE ABOUT GOD

God in Guru Granth Sahib is referred to in terms of human relations as father, mother, brother, relative, friend, lover and husband. Other names of God in His supremacy are Thakur, Prabhu, Swami, Shah, Patshah, Sahib and Sain. Some traditional names are Ram, Narayan, Govind, Gopal, Allah and Khuda. Some positive terms related to God are Dataa, Dataar, Kartaa, Kartaar, Dyaal, Kirpal, Qadir and Qarim. Some names peculiar to Sikhism are Naam, Sabad and Waheguru which stand for Divine or Supreme Being. Every human being forgets but God and the Guru is beyond forgetfulness:

"Bhullan andar sabh ko abhul Guru Karataar." p-535

God is my protector. He is the knower of the secrets of every heart:

"Rakha ek hamaara Swaami. Sagal ghtaan ka antarjamee." p-1136

God, the creator and sustainer of this universe gives to man what He planned to give him to keep him advancing in life towards Him. Even for a child, milk is produced in the mother's body before the child is born. He provides food for the small insects even in stones. Gurbani says that God is the greatest provider and we eat what He provides us:

"Toon Dataa Dataar Tera ditaa khaavna." p-652

Off all the beings in this world there is only one provider (God). Let me not forget Him:

"Sabhnaa jeaan ka ik daataa so meh visar naa jaaee." p-2

Nanak says that Har (God) is father and mother of all in this world and we are His children. He is taking care of us:

"Nanak pitaa maataa hai Har Prabh hum baarik Har pritpaaray." p-882

God likes to hear it as praises when some body is doing meditation on Him:

"Gobind bhaao bhagat da bhukhaa." - Bhaee Gurdaas

17

God likes it as His own praise when one of His Saints is praised in public:

"Har aapnee vadiadee bhavadee jan ka jaikaar kraa-ay." p-652

God is the originator of all music and loves it. At the entrance to Sach Ghar (house of True God) there is much music from so many musical instruments and so many fairies are playing the instruments. There are so many singers and so many raagas being sung for God:

"Vaajay naad anek asankhaa kete tere vaavanharey
Kete raag pari sio kaheeay kete Tere gavanhaare." p-6

All these raagas are played in the sound current of naad (mystical sound) and are true. One cannot put any price on these:

"Raag naad sabh sach hain keemat kahee na jaa-ay." p-1423

He loves singing hymns by His Bhagats, praising Him on His door:

"Bhagat tere mun bhanvde dar sohan kirtan gaanvde." p-233

He creates and takes care of the baby in the mother's womb. How can we forget Him:

"Maata ke udder meh pritpaal kare so kio mano vissariay." p-920

Intelligence and understanding is given by God to man. Guru Ji tells that there is no foolish or wise man. God's Will determines so:

"Naa ko moorakh naa ko sianaa.
Varte sabh kish tera bhana." p-98

Our knowledge, understanding and intelligence are determined by God. I know only what God informs me to know, Lord:

"Surat matt chaturaee Teri, Too jana-ay jaanaa Ram." p-779

God takes care of us even when we are in our mother's womb. He protects His people in all places as a father and mother. Our birth and death is determined by His Will. What we do in this life is by His Will and what is best for us is by His Will. But we talk of a free will and do things the way we like, but suffer in the end. It is told in the first hymn of Guru Granth Sahib that we have to follow His Will, Nanak says:

"Hukam rjaee challnaa Nanak likhiaa naal." p-1

We have no power to do anything at all. As it pleases You, You forgive us all:

"Assan jor naheen je kich kar hum saaken jion bhaave tion baksh." p-730

God lovingly embraces whoever comes to His sanctuary; this the way of The Lord and Master:

"Jo saran aavay tis kanth laavay eh bird Swaamy sanda." p-544

I serve the Lord by chanting the Name of God:

"Har ki tehl kmaavanee jappeeay Har ka Naaon." p-300

Even the ones ungrateful to Him are taken care of by God, O Nanak. He is forever the Forgiver:

"Akirtghana noon palda Prabh Nanak sud bakhsand." p-47

God automatically does the work of those who love the Naam of the Lord:

"Achint kam kare Prabh tinke jin Har kaa Naam piaaraa." p-635

Those who serve God find peace and bliss; they are intuitively absorbed into God's Naam:

"Jin Har seviaa tinn sukh paaiaa.
Sehje hee Har Naam smaayaa." p-11

There is so much to be written about God in Guru Granth Sahib that one can go on forever. He has given us an infinite universe, a life and has a complete responsibility and control over it for us to be happy if we live by His Will in His world. This is the only way we can be with Him, our Father and Mother, and have peace and bliss infinitely by merging with Him. We will never to be born again unless He Wills it for us to serve Him in the physical world wherever and whenever He wants.

CREATION OF UNIVERSE

We are all very curious to know as to how this universe came into being and we seek answers. Our religious scriptures answer this query by saying all creation was done by God. God also controls and runs it per His own plan and nothing is out of His Will. However, scientists have put forward their own theories that the universe came into being after a big-bang of a huge solid mass billions of years ago. They believe that what we see now is a natural result of that explosion and evolution with time. But what was the source of that huge solid mass and why did it explod? They have not explained it yet. Let us examine how Guru Granth Sahib Ji, the Sikh Holy Scripture, explains the formation of this universe from the very beginning.

Guru Nanak, the founder of Sikh religion tells us that God created this universe in many ways and means:

"Nanak rachna Prabh rachee bauh bidh anak parkaar." p-275

All creation came into being under God's order:

"Hukmi hovan akaar." p-1

Let us first consider the physical creation which covers galaxies, solar systems, star, planets, moons with air, water, heat and skies. There is only One God, a formless infinite spiritual Creator Being who is beyond time, omnipresent, omnipotent, true forever and self existent and with no attributes. In His deep divine silence as He planned to express Himself in attributes, Heuttered One Word and universe started taking shape:

"Keeta psaao eko kwaao." p-3

The Word He uttered carried His Plan, His Will or Hukam, His Power of Creation and His Own self in it. This Word is also called His Sabad or Naam in Gurbani:

"Eko Naam Hukam hai." p-72

Creation and destruction takes place with His Sabad and then creation takes place again by His Sabad:

"Uttpatt parlo sabday hovay.
Sabday he phir opatt hoavy." p-117

Naam created galaxies and planets. And Naam created the skies and the nether worlds. Naam also is responsible for all of His creation:

"Naam kay dhaaray khand brahmand.
Naam kay dhaaray agaas pataal." p-284
"Naamay he tay sabh kich hoa." p-753

Now how do these physical creations come into being? God sitting in sunn or His divine silence created five subtle basic components of creation (air, water, earth, fire and sky):

"Panch tutt sunno pargaasa." p-1036

God used these five subtle components or essences to create the universe:

"Panch tutt kar tudh srist sabh saajee." p-736

First The True One created air, and from air created water, and from water He created the other components. He created the three worlds in air on earth and in sea (with life present in all of them) with His Jot sitting in each of them:

"Saachay tay pavna bhaiaa pavnay tay jal hoay.
Jal tay traiy bhavan saajiaa ghat ghat Jot smoay." p-19

Air, water and fire (heat) were present in the darkness within the great fog. This fog stayed on for millions of years. There was no earth or sky, everything stayed as it was under God's command. There was no day or night, neither moon nor sun, God stayed in His deep silence:

"Arbad narbad dhundookaaraa.
Dharan naa gaganaa hukam appaaraa.
Na din raen naa chand na sooraj sunn smadh lagaainda." p-1035

God sat alone unaffected in this absolute dark fog, the world of conflicts did not exist yet:

"Dhundookaar Niraalam baithaa naa tad dhund psaaraa hai." p-1026

This dark fog lasted for thirty-six ages (each age is supposed to be hundreds of thousands of years as mentioned in ancient scriptures). Then He decided to reveal Himself in His creation. He created the world and gave consciousness to all:

"Chattees jug gubaar saa aapay ganat keeni.
Aappay srist sabh saaj aap mutt denee." p-949

When God willed He created the world. Without any supporting pillars He put the universe in place:

"Jaa tis bhaanaa taa jagat upaaiaa.
Bajh kalaa udaan rkhaaiaa." p-1036

How are all of the celestial creations in place without any support? Gurbani explains that it is held in place by the very Sabad or celestial sound which created these. This is mentioned in the following line in Gurbani. When the wandering mind stopped, it met the Satguru (within) who helped it reach the tenth door (entrance to our spiritual home). There the spiritual food, 'sehaj dhun' the music of Anhad Sabad goes on all the time and this is the Sabad which is holding the entire world in place:

"Dhavat thamiaa Satgur miliaa daswaan duaar paaiaa.
Tithay amrit bhojan sehaj dhun upjay jit sabad jagat sabh thum rkhaiaa." p-441

God formed the planets and the solar systems, nether regions and Himself invisible to the eyes. He manifested Himself in His creation:

"Khand mandal pataal arambhay gupto pargat aindaa." p-1036

Millions of fields of creatures and planets are born. Millions of skies and countless galaxies are created:

"Kaee kot khanee aur khand.
Kaee kot akaash brahmand." p-276

So many ways He has unfolded Himself. So many times He has expanded His creation:

"Kaee jugat keeno bisthaar.
Kaee baar pasrio psaar." p-276

As He wills He creates the world. When He so wills He pulls it all unto Himself again:

"Ja tis bhaavay taa srist upaa-ay.
Apnay bhaanay la-ay smaa-ay." p-292

People often guess about the time of creation of the universe, but Guru Ji does not specify any time. The day or date of creation is not known to Yogees nor does anyone else know about the season or month of creation. Only the Creator of the universe knows about it:

"Thitt vaar na jogi jaanay rutt mah na koay.
Ja karta sristi ko saajay aapay janay soay." p-4

ANHAD SABAD

Anhad means continuous or nonstop. Sabad in Gurbani means the utterance of God. Thus, Anhad Sabad translates to the Continuous Divine Utterance, which was first uttered by God and is still going on in the universe. It is not an utterance in the physical sense where sound is produced by striking two material objects together. That sound eventually dies as the energy that produced it is used up fighting the resistance of the media in which it travels. Contrarily, Anhad Sabad started in sunn, the materially void infinite space, and is still present in sunn which encloses the whole universe: "Antar sunnun bahar sunnum tribhavan sunmsunum" p-943. It is this Sabad that created the universe: "Ek kwaa-ay te sab hoaa" p-1002 and it is with this Sabad that it is destroyed and created again:

"Utput parlo sabday hovay.
Sabday he phir opat hovay." p-117

God is fully expressed in Anhad Sabad, which is also called Naam in Gurbani. Naam carries in it the Divine Hukam/Will, Divine Plan of creation, preservation and destruction, Divine Intelligence/Wisdom/ Consciousness, Divine Laws and everything that God is. Naam created everything and is in everything: "Jetta keeta tetta Naaon. Vin Naavain naheen ko thaaon" p-4. Naam, or Anhad Sabad, persists in every creation of God as a Soul. So God extends into us as Sabad or Naam. Guru Nanak calls this Sabad as His Guru: "Sabad Guru surat dhun chela" p-943 and calls his own surti, or consciousness, as Sabad's disciple. It is through this Sabad that Guru Nanak advises us to use to connect to God. God is speaking in all our bodies through this Sabad:

"Sabhay ghat Ram bolay." p-988
"Ghat ghat vaajay Naad." p-6

It is this Sabad that Gurbani is advising us to connect to so we can hear our Creator or Father. And it is with this Sabad that we link with Naam which cleans our mind so we can connect with God Himself. Without this Sabad everybody is in spiritual darkness and Sabad enlightens the mind:

"Jeean andar jeeo Sabad hai jit Sauh milaavaa ho-ay.
Bin Sabday jag anher hai Sabdey pargat ho-ay." p-1250

Sabad can be heard by taking our consciousness inside where it resides in the body. The only way to do it is to silence our mind from its thoughts of the physical world of Maya. Naam Japna is the means to do that. This is accomplished by a cyclic utterance of Gurmantar and listening to it attentively till our surti is lost into the chant of it. Once we disconnect from our thoughts and land into a mentally quiet state, which Gurbani calls sunn, where Naam and Sabad reside. Even a short experience in that state is very relaxing and peaceful. If performed in the company of experienced practitioners one will soon start hearing Anhad Sabad in one's ears (it can be mistaken for a tinnitus problem). The sounds generally heard are: ringing of bells, flutes, chirping of birds in the morning, crickets in nature in the evening, rebabs, sitars, drums, your own heart beat, etc.

These sounds when heard in a state of sunn is a direct link to Sabad or Naam. Our mind is then cleansed of the dirt of Maya and gets closer to higher spiritual stages. We are advised to hear these Sabads:

"Mun dhovo Sabad laago Har sio raho chit laa-ay." p-919

Hearing Sabad is like bathing the mind in a pool of nectar of Naam or Amritsar. Guru Ji advises every Sikh to do Naam Japna in the early morning hours and wash their mind by bathing it in Amritsar:

Gur Satgur ka jo Sikh akha-ay so bhalkay uth Hari Naam dhiaavay. Udam karay bhalkay parbhaatee isnaan karay Amritsar nhaavay." p-305

The mind is further cleansed by regular Japna and will start hearing Sehaj Dhun - a high frequency, sharp, low volume note which continues all the time. This happens when mind reaches third sunn or dasam duaar or the doorway to enter the divine mansion. At that point all other nine doors of the body are closed and the tenth one is reached where Anhad Sabad goes on day and night and is heard by following the Guru's advice:

"Nau dar thaakay dhaavat raha-ay. Dasvain nij ghar vaasaa paa-ay. Othay Anhad Sabad vajay din raatee. Gurmatee Sabad sunaavaniaa." p-124

When the time comes for union with God, Anhad Sabad changes to Toor (the sound of a long horn that is played outside Gurdwaras and temples): "Binvant Nanak Gur charan laagay vaajay Anhad Tooray" p-917, followed by Naad, a loud low frequency, humming sound before you are let into Sach Ghar or the Divine Mansion: "Anhad Banee Naad vjaaia" p-375. When the mind makes its entry into Sach Ghar, Anhad Sabad changes to Panch Shabad which welcomes the child of God to His House, Who is the Emperor of the entire universe:

"Vaajay panch Shabad titt ghar subhaagay." p-917

Mind then is fully awakened to its spiritual self by the Sabad:

"Dhun upjee Sabad jgaaia." p-1039

Free from bondage of Maya, the mind sees nothing but Parkaash or Divine Light/Jot and finally meets the Beloved Lord:

"Pargati Jot milay Ram Piaray." p-375

This happens with the Grace of the Guru (Sabad Guru and Gurbani Guru) and the mind finds peace and tranquility in the Divine Company:

"Gur Nanak tuthaa miliaa Har Raaiaa.
Sukh raen vihaani sehaj subhaaiaa." p-375

The stage above is the Fourth Sunn, or Anhad Sunn, and the end of the mind's journey back to its true home, Nij Ghar. Here it can live in perfect peace and bliss as Jiwan Mukat, which means to be liberated while alive. The mind becomes just like the One Who created him:

"Anhad sunn rattay se kaisay.
Jistay upjay tis he jaisay." p-943

Such minds become Gurmukh/spiritual and they have easy access from Bhavjal Sagar to Nij Ghar and back via sunn and Anhad Sabad:

"Gurmukh aavay jaa-ay nisang." p -932

These liberated minds are given different assignments by God to spend the rest of their life in service to other people as Sants, Sadhus, Bhagats and Brahm Gianis discussed in an another missive.

The House of Satguru Nanak has thus offered a simple and easy way to achieve salvation, be free from the cycle of birth and death, and freedom from all the grief linked with it. We are very lucky to have this knowledge and guidance in Gurbani and Sadh Sangat to achieve the human life's mission of gaining ultimate freedom/spirituality.

Let us all thank Satguru Ji and follow his advice to become Gurmukhs.

Naam is the spiritual extension of God Himself within His creation. It can only be perceived as being spiritual in nature as it is beyond our intellectual grasp. Naam was God's first creation through which He formed the rest of the universe that we are a part of. It lies within us, yet we do not know or understand it. The entire focus of Gurbani is to connect us with the Naam within us so we can realize ourselves and our Creator, God, and achieve salvation and bliss. Often, Naam is confused with the Name of God. Naam isn't the name; it is God Himself within His created universe. Given below is a very brief write up on Naam as I understood it from Gurbani, some Gurmukhs and personal experience.

NAAM

Naam is a Divine Consciousness, Wisdom, Intelligence, Creative Power, Plan, Will, Order (Hukam), Light (Jyot), Utterance (Sabad), Love, Grace, etc. It is everything that God is. So it is the essence of God (Siv) and His extension into Maya (Sakti) and His creation, both physically visible and invisible.

God created Naam out of Himself. He used Naam to create His universe and is sitting in each of His creations as Naam and is relishing it:

"Appeenay aap saajio aapeenay rachio Naaon.
Dooee kudrat saajeeay kar assan ditho chaao." p-463

Naam, which was His first creation, is like God in that it is true or pure for ever:

"Sat Naam." p-1

God created this universe with His one utterance (bol or kvaao):

"Keeeta psaao eko kwaao" p-3
"Ek kwaao tay sabh hoaa." p-1003

Utterance of God in Gurbani is called Sabad. It is His Sabad which contains Naam. Guru Ji uses Naam and Sabad in Gurbani for the same entity. Both Naam and Sabad are said to be responsible for creation and destruction:

"Utpat parlo sabday hovay." p-117
"Naamay he tay sabh kich hooa." p-753

It is through Sabad that we connect with Naam and through Sabad again we unite with God:

"Sabday he Naaon upjay Sabday mail milaaiaa." p-644

Whatever He did was through His Naam:

"Jetta keetta ttetta Naao." p-4

Like the nine most precious jewels, Naam is sitting inside our bodies as the Divine Nectar:

"Nau nidh Amrit Prabh ka Naam.
Dehi meh iskaa bisraam." p-293

God's Jyot or Light shines in each of our bodies and gives it life:

"Sabh meh Jyot Jyot hai Soay.
Tisde chanan sabh meh chanan hoay." p-643

God speaks in each of our bodies and there is no other than God who speaks there:

"Sabhay ghat Ram bolay Rama bolay.
Ram bina ko bolay ray." p-988

Naam is what Guru Ji calls Atma of Parmaatmaa residing within us and keeping us alive. When this Naam/Atma or soul/swan leaves, the body falls dead. A wife can get scared of a dead body and run away calling it a ghost:

"Atam Ram Ram hai Atam." p-1030
"Jab eh huns taji eh kaaiaa pret pret kar bhaagee." p-634

It is Naam or Sabad what Guru Nanak Dev Ji calls his Guru and his surat (consciousness) as its disciple:

"Sabad Guru surat dhun chela." p-943

Misunderstanding this Sabad as Gurbani, most current scholars are calling Sri Guru Granth Sahib as Shabad Guru whereas it is Sabad Guru/Gurbani Guru/Satguru. In Gurbani, the words Guru and Satguru refer to Naam or God and not the physical Guru Jis themselves. Guru Ji considers Naam and God the same:

"Gur Govind Govind Guru hai Nanak bhed na bhaee." p-442

Why don't we hear or see Naam? Because we don't make an effort to take our surat (or consciousness) into our bodies with a purpose to see it. The only thing we have to do is to sing or make a 'dhun' of the name of God which is the Gurmantra, Waheguru, given to us by Guru Ji. By reciting the Gurmantra again and again while listening attentively to it without thinking anything else, we will hear and see Naam. Guru Ji calls it Naam Japna and advises us to do it in a cyclical manner with our breathing (saas graass, saas saas japna) till surti goes inside. This condition is called Samadhi (of the body) and sunn (the thoughtless mind) in Gurbani. In sunn we cannot do any Japna as the body is in Samadhi. It is in this sunn that Naam or God can be reached as they also live in sunn:

"Sunn samaadh gufa teh aasan kewal Brahm pooran teh baasan."
p-894

The best way to understand and do japna is in the company of true
saints:

"Sadhu sang bhajo Gopal." p-675

Guru Ji advises us to go into sunn (sunn/samadhi) by listening
attentively (in dhyan) to the dhun of Gurmantra and then only you
can know or hear Him or see Him:

"Dhun meh dhyaan dhyaan meh jaanyaa." p-879

When the mind goes inside where Naam is, it starts to be cleansed
by it:

"Bhareeay mutt paapaan ke sang O dhpoay Naavay kay rung." p-4

One day, when the mind is cleansed enough, it will start hearing the
Sabad which means one has established a link with Naam. More such
cleansing will make the mind clean enough that one can see the Light
of Naam and become ready to see Him. He is the light of countless
suns, when all the doubts and spiritual darkness/duality will vanish
(and one becomes ready for the union with Akal Purakh):

"Naam japat kot soor ujiaara binsay bharam andheraa." p-700

God, Naam, and Sabad all belong to the zone of sunn and one has to
take the mind into that zone by japna of the Gurmantra. Japna ends
when surti goes into sunn where the rest is in the hands of the Sabad/
Naam Guru. The first experience of sunn may last five to ten minutes
and may increase to an hour or more. The mind, when cleansed, starts
accumulating the wealth of Naam. The mind then becomes richer and
higher in spirituality when the five doots of Maya begin to lose their
grip on the mind. In the end they not only lose their grip but become

the servants of mind, as they were in the beginning. The mind is set free from Maya by Naam, the grief caused by the five doots of Maya, and it conquers death forever. Thus the mind becomes jivan-mukat or free of death, never to be born again:

"Panch doot tudh vus keetay Kaal kantak maaria." p-917

Sabad and Naam is the way to our Creator Being, Karta Purakh. Gurbani stresses on Naam in every hymn we read. The way to connect with Naam is through Sabad, and we connect with Sabad through Naam Japna; this connection is the first and foremost duty of a Sikh:

"Gur Satgur ka jo Sikh akhavay.
So bhalkay uth Hari Naam dhiaavay." p-305

Without Naam the whole world is insane or out of their true mind. Only a Gurmukh knows the truth:

"Bin Naanvay jug kamlaa phiray Gurmukh nadri aaia." p-643

Cursed is living in the world without having secured Naam of the True One in your heart:

"Dhrig jeevan sansar Sachay Naam bin." p-956

Your Naam O God is the destroyer of all grief:

"Har Har teraa Naam hai dukh metanhaaraa." p-725

MAYA

Right after Sabad, which is used as Anhad Sabad in the Sri Guru Granth Sahib and misinterpreted as Gurbani, Maya is the second most misunderstood word in Gurbani. Here is some input on Maya which may help to clarify the subject. It is the world of Maya we live in; it is Maya which leads us into problems. It is Maya we have to fight against to win freedom and to gain union with God. Guru Ji has referred to and discussed this subject quite often to make us understand it.

Maya is all the visible creation of God we live in. God put the world of Maya to work as per His plan. But He installed in the minds an intoxicating love for the world and led the whole world astray:

"Tudh aapai jagat upaaeykai appey dhandhe laeyaa.
Moh thagauly paaeykai tudh apau jagat bhulaaeaa." p-138

However, Maya is not an objective reality and leads to duality rather than unity; so like a mirage, the world becomes an end in itself. Maya's game lasts only a few days. Blinded by Maya man forgets Naam. He neither obtains Naam nor Maya after physical death:

"Baba Maya rachna dhoh.
Andhe Naam visaariaa naa tis eh naa oh." p-5

Maya is what makes you forget God and produces attachments to the world and duality:

"Eh Maya jit Har visre moh upje bhao dooja laaiaa." p-921

The heat of the womb within the mother's body is like the fire of Maya outside. The fire of Maya and heat of the womb are all the same. The creator has set up this play in action:

"Jaisee agan udar meh taisee bahar Maya.
Maya agan sabh iko jehi Karte khel rachaiaa." p-921

Maya entices the human mind with temporary pleasures and gains, but let's it down. Only the rare ones understand it:

"Baba Maya saath na hoay.
In Maya jag mohiaa virlaa boojhay koay." p-595

Life under the influence of Maya totally blinds the mind to its own reality. Mind neither sees its own spirituality nor hears the non-struck melody of Naam and makes uproar and tumult for nothing:

"Mayadharee utt annaah bola.
Shabad naa sunaee bauh raul ghcholaa." p-313

Maya influences the mind in three modes (gunas). Each mode has its own characteristics based on its source, the element it is made of:

1. Rajas Mode is based on the element air, creates hopes, ambitions, anxieties, etc.
2. Satvic Mode is based on the element water, creates kindness, contentment, sense of duty (dharma), discipline, charity, etc.
3. Tamsic Mode based on the element fire, creates lust, anger, greed, attachment, ego, duality, hatred, slandering, etc:

    "Raj gun tum gun satt gun kaheeay.
    Eh teri sub Maya." p-1123

Life thus spent under the three modes of Maya is called life in 'Bhavjal Sagar' or 'Horrifying Ocean of the World' (it will be referred to as Ocean of Maya).

In Satyug when human life began, the mind was pure like a golden swan, being born out of the Pure One, God. In Duapper and Tretta Yug (each yug of time spans of over hundreds of thousands of years) the mind became more human, tainted with Maya and only the rare ones could control their ego. In the present age of Kalyug, minds have become like goblins except for those who have already realized God:

"Kal meh pret jinni Ram na pachata.
Satyug param huns beechari.
Duappar trette maanas warte.
Virle haume maaree." p-1131

Thus many a life time is lost in hatred, enmity, lust, attachment, falsehood, wasteful deeds, deep greed and deceit:

"Bair birodh kaam krodh moh.
Jhooth bikaar mahaan lobh dhroh.
Ihaoon jugat bihaane kaee janam." p-267

Mind has thus become so polluted with filth of the above vices that no divine light can filter through it:

"Janam janam ki is mun kau mal laagee kala hoaa siah." p-651

Mind is thus lost in the Ocean of Maya and forgotten its own home, the 'Nij Ghar'. Feeding on vices, worries and anxieties all the time it has forgotten that its true food is nectar of Naam:

"Mun ka tossa Hari Naam hai." p-756

The polluted mind sees everything full of filth. Washing the body does not cleanse the mind. The whole world is deluded by doubts and hardly anyone understands this. By following the yogic postures of Siddhas one may control lust, but it still does not cleanse the mind of filth or eliminate the ego:

"Mun mailey sub kuch maila tun dhote mun hacchaa no hoey.
Eh jagat bharam bhulaya virlaa boojhay koay.

Sidhaan ke assan sikhe indri vuss kar kamaa-ay.
Mun ki mail naa uttrey haumey mail naa jaaay." p-558

Therefore, it is the three gunas of Maya which pollute the mind and lures it away from God. The remedy for its cleansing is given by Guru Ji in SGGS: detaching the mind away from Maya by connecting it to Naam through Naam Japna/Simran/Dhiauna, honest earning of our livelihood, and sharing our material wealth with others. The advice is repeated again and again so that it can sink in our mind and take effect one day, provided we read Gurbani. Naam cleanses the mind and makes it ready for the vision and union with God when the control of the five doots of Maya is lost. The doots then become servants of the mind. A Jivan Mukat mind, a mind in union with God, lives in spiritual bliss and doesn't have to be born in another body again. Just as Naam saves the baby in the mother's womb: "Maat garabh maen apna simran deh tai Tum rakhanhare" p-613, so does it save the mind in the outside world and brings it back to its original spiritual self. I end here with many thanks to Guru Ji for showing us the way to peace and happiness.

HUKAM

In Gurbani, Hukam is the Creator of God's Will or Order by which He creates, controls and runs His creation and actions of the creatures. The entire creation took place by His Will and nobody can speak of His Will: "Hukmee hovan akaar hukam na kahiaa jaaee." p-1. The entire creation is under His control and nothing is out of it: "Hukmay andar sabhko baahar Hukam na ko-ay" p-1. Whatever happens in this world is by His Will:

"Jio jioTera hukam tivay tiv hovna." p-523

All live beings and their bodies are created by God and they work according to what He planned for them. All that happens is by His Will and nothing here is our doing:

"Jee jant sabh tudh upaa-ay.
Jit jit bhaanaa tit tit laa-ay.
Sabh kich keeta Teraa hoay nahee kich asaadaa jeeo." p-103

Creation started taking place by God's one Sabad/utterance:

"Keeta psaao ekay kwaao." p-3

By His Sabad He creates, by His Sabad He destroys it and by His Sabad He creates it again:

"Utpat parlo Sabday hovay.

Sabday he phir opat hovay." p-117

Sabad is the source of life in all live beings. And it is through this Sabad that the Jeev can meet with their Creator:
"Jeeaan andar jeeo Sabad hai jit Sauh milaavaa hovay." p-1250

The self-existing God created Naam from within Himself, out of that He created the physical world in which He sits as Naam and is enjoying His creation:

"Aapeenay aap saajio aapeenay rachio Naao.
Dooee kudrat saajio kar aasan ditho chaao." p-463

Naam /Sabad in live beings is the Atma/Soul or the Parmatma/God: "Atam Ram Ram hai Atam." The Divine illumination of God is called Jot in Gurbani. This Jot is in every live being because of His presence as Atma in every live being:

"Sabh meh Jot Jot hai Soay." p-663

God's Hukam lies in Naam/Sabad. Nanak has been told this by the Satguru/Soul:

"Eka Naam hukam hai Nanak Satgur deea bhujhaa-ay jio." p-72

God carries out His Hukam through Naam. To understand His Hukam our mind should meditate on Him to connect with Naam (which lies within us): "Nau nidh amrit Prabh ka Naam.
Dehi meh iskaa bisraam." p-293

"So aisa Har Naam dhiaaeeay mun meray.
Jo sabhnaan oopar hukam chlaa-ay." p-80

Connected with Naam (through japna), we understand His Hukam that leads to the realization God:

"Kauh Nanak jin Hukam pchhattaa. Prabh Sahib kaa tin bhaid jaataa"
p-885

Knowing Him we realize that everything is in God's control and that we have no power to do anything by ourselves and we do whatever He wills:

"Meray Har jio sabh ko teray vuss.
Assaan jor naheen jay kich kar hum saakayn jio bhaavay tio baksh."
p-735

Deeds we perform as per our destiny that God has written for us:

"Jaisa likhat likhiaa dhur Kartay hum taiseee kirat kmaa-ee." p-882

Till we realize that His Hukam (that everything is happening by His Will), we suffer. But once we realize His Will by the help of the Guru we are relieved of these sufferings:

"Jab lag Hukam na boojhta tab he lau dukhia.
Gur mil hukam pashaania tab he lai sukhiaa." p-400

A manmukh, self willed person, is blind to His Hukam and depends on his own intellectual cleverness. He never understands His Will and suffers:

"Manmukh andh karay chaturaee.
Bhaanaa naa manay bauhat dukh paee." p-1064

Once we realize His Will and accept it, we are accepted in His Divine Mansion (becoming jeevan mukat):

"Hukam maneeay hovay parvaan ta Khasmay kaa Mehal paa-aysee."
p-471

It is under His Will that we go through a cycle of reincarnations and is by His grace that we are rid of that. It is through His Will that we bear sufferings and it is under His Will we do whatever deeds He plans for us to do:

"Bahanay jon bhvaaee-ay bhaanay bakash karay.
Bhaanay dukh sukh bhogee-ay bhaanay karam karay." p-963

By His Will we are born here and by His Will we leave (die) or meet Him. It is by His Will that we create this web of physical lures and attachments and relish the pleasures of all our senses (and suffer):

"Hukmay jag meh aa-iaa chalan Hukam sanjog jio.
Hukmay parpanch psaa-ria hukam karay ras bhog jio." p-760

It is obvious from above that our life is running under God's Will whether we know His Will or not. We are happy when we come to know His Will and accept it. But we suffer when we do not know His Will and blame everybody else for our sufferings which are due to our karmas of the past and current life: "Mastak likhia lekh purab kmaa-ia jio" p-689. This destiny was written by God's Will:

"Nanak hukmee likhia lekh." p-466

The entire universe is created by God under His control and is supported by His Sabad/Naam. This is revealed in the following statement of Gurbani that 'when the mind stops its wandering it meets Satguru it reaches the spiritual gate (The tenth Door) that opens for it. Where the divine food of sehaj dhun, a divine melody goes on that is supporting the entire world in place under God's Will':

"Dhavat thamiaan Satgur mileeay daswaan dwaar paaiaa.
Tithay amrit bhojan sehaj dhun upjay tis sabad jagat sabh thum rakhaa-ia." p-440

We, the humans, have come to know a little bit about the infinite physical universe of God's creation. Out of this understanding have framed certain laws about the forces working within this universe, which we have come across by accident or by investigation using the intelligence given to us by God Himself: "Sikh matt sabh budh tumari" p-795. These laws have helped us in creating tools and equipment that have provided more material comforts to us here. Now there is all this focus on material comforts and a total neglect on our spiritual needs of our mind, whose food is Naam: "Mun ka tosa Hari Naam hai." p-756. Our mind is now being fed by the five doots of Maya (lust, anger, greed, attachments and ego) resulting in high stress in anything we do in life. It looks like the world is sitting on the brink of war. This war, if nuclear, will be the last war as only a few will be left to fight another.

These laws of Nature are man-made and based on the forces of Nature made by God. Man has started abusing these forces for selfish ends. These laws are Mayan forces which are only a part of God's plan to run the universe. God can change these laws whenever He wants to do whatever He wills with the world He created. It is His Will to keep this world or destroy it. This He has done many a time before: "Kaee baar pasrio paasaar." p-276. He creates all of this using the five subtle elements (air, water, fire, earth and sky). It is the air element which keeps all the others together in its form. Whenever God wants He can pull the air out and everything will crumble to no form, leaving the subtle elements behind:

"Pavnay khail keea sabh thaaeen kalaa khinch dhhaainda." p-1033

God run this universe by His spiritual command which is called His Hukam. Gurmukhs understand His Hukam and live in it. This is what pleases God and such persons have no obstacles in life:

"Prabh bhaanaa apnaa bhavdaa jis bakhshay tis bighan naa koay." p-1258

*Here is a brief introduction to the human mind as advised by Gurbani
and some Gurmukhs. We are in essence our mind, who is the child of
God, and is sent on a physical journey on this planet as a participant
in God's Play. As part of His plan, the mind forgets its true identity
by getting lured into the physical world and suffers by not finding the
true happiness. The True Guru advises it to find its way back through
Naam. Till it finds its way back to its true home it keeps on coming
back into bodies and going through a cycle of births and deaths due
to its attachments to the physical world and its ego.*

MIND

We often talk about our mind but only have a very vague idea about
what it is. People generally think the mind is just a bundle of thoughts
or perhaps it is the brain. Even talking to some psychiatrists and
psychologists who were making their living on this being called the
mind, I found they did not have a clear picture about it. Christian
and Jewish preachers talk of the soul as a good soul or a bad soul
and not the mind. But the soul is part of God and it is pure, so how
could it be bad? It must be perfect like God. Generally, we associate
the mind with our body. When asked, 'Who are you?', the answer
mostly is their name. When told, 'It is your name. But who are you?'
They show their ID and when questioned again the answer generally
is 'Don't you see me? I am standing right in front of you.' This
means that they identify themselves to be their body. Whose body
that is, they still do not know. It is only in Sri Guru Granth Sahib
that our real identity is explained. Even after reading and hearing the
recitation of SGGS many a time, we are still not aware of the answer
or perhaps we never cared to look for it. I will try to discuss it here
as I understand it from Guru Ji and the Gurmukhs, who have gained

the spiritual knowledge of Gurbani from the Sabad Guru. The Sabad Guru resides inside each one of us, but only the lucky ones meet with Him with His grace:

"Sabh meh Sabad vartay Prabh Sacha karam milay bialun." p-1275

Gurbani talks about God and His creation. It advises us about our life here on Earth and it often directly addresses our mind: "Mun re kaun kumatt tai leeny", "Mun mere karte noo salaah", "Eh mun meria too sada rhau Har naalay", "Naach re mun Gur ke aage," "Jaag re mun jagan haaray," so on. So, the real part of us is the mind. The mind is also called 'jeev' in Gurbani. Jeev is the live being who is residing in this body. Now who is this jeev? Gurbani tell us "Kauh Kabir eh Raam ki uns" p-871. It is the child of God. Guru Ji tells us again that the mind is the personification of Jot, the Light of God, "Mun too Jot saroop hain apnaa mool pachaan" p-411. The mind is told to realize its origin. In fact the main focus of the Gurbani is to guide and help the mind to know its origin, God, and be united with Him. God created the mind in 'Saram Khand', one of the Khands mentioned in Japji Sahib. "Tithe ghariay surat matt mun budh." The mind is provided with consciousness, 'matt', its basic nature as a human, and intelligence which it has to use while living in the world where it is sent. Like all other creatures of God, the mind has been sent to this physical planet Earth, called Dharti /Maat Lok in Gurbani, and hence is given a physical body. For the human it is given the body through human parents. However, the mind comes in its own subtle body which houses the soul too; "Sookham moorat Naam Niranjan kayan ka akaar" p-466. Naam Niranjan here stands for soul. This subtle body is tied inside the human body at a point below the belly button called 'dharan' or 'mool duaar': "Mool duaaray bandhia bandh" p-1159. So the mind is attached to this body but its consciousness can move around wherever it wants.

The mind, although a Jot of God, is under the influence of all five components of creation, which are air, water, fire, earth and sky, and Maya. The mind creates itself a Mayan personality to interact with the material world and perform all the actions and duties through the body: "Eh mun karman eh mun dharma eh mun punch tutt te janmaa" p-415. The mind lands into this physical body which is formed of these five components of Maya in a gross physical form.

That is where it makes its first contact with visible Maya: "Eh sareer sabh mool hai maya" p-1065 and the mind falls for it. It is influenced by the three gunas or qualities or modes of Maya: Raj Gun, Tum Gun and Sat Gun. Rajas mode creates hopes, ambitions, anxieties and worries, etc. Tamas mode creates lust, anger, greed, attachment, ego, duality, hatred and slandering, etc. Satvic mode creates kindness, contentment, sense of duty, discipline, charity, etc. Life under the influence of these modes of Maya is called a life in 'Bhavjal Sagar'. Rajas and tamas mode pollute the mind and it cannot think of reality of its spiritual nature and turns away from God. The only way to stop its pollution is to spend time under the satvic mode, working honestly and being content in the rajas mode, while completely avoiding the tamas mode. The polluted mind can further be cleansed by Naam, the spiritual power of God:

"Bhariay matt paapaan ke sang oh dhopay naavay ke rung." p-4

Being a child of God, the mind is briefed by God before it lands here on earth to be careful of the three doots of Maya. Tum Gun (lust, anger, greed, attachment and ego) are there to serve the mind but can take control over it. So, take protection under the illumination of Sabad (Naam) whenever the mind goes out of the body: "Panch paharvaa dar peh rehtay inkaa naheen patiaara. Chet suchet chit hoay rhau lai parkaash ujaara" p-339. The mind is also given intelligence and 'matt', its basic nature as a human: "Sikh matt sabh budh tumari" p-795. The mind is supposed to use this intelligence for achieving the goal for which the human body is given to do. That goal is to break away from the hold of Maya and attain union with God, "Bhae prapat manukh dehuia Gobind Milan kee ehee teri baria" p-12. Serving the Master, God, with true intelligence wins the mind respect in this world and in His Court: "Akli Sahib seveeay akli paaeeay maan." p-1245. But what happens is that under the influence of Maya, the mind forgets the advice and many a life time are wasted in hatred, enmity, attachments, falsehood, wasteful deeds, deep greed and deceit:

"Bair birodh kaam krodh moh. Jhooth bikaar mahaan lobh dhroh. Ehaoon jugat bihaanay kaee janam." p-258

Life on this planet for the mind is limited by time and the number of breaths allowed for the body. This limit cannot be changed and is allocated at the time of birth of the body: "Gin ghale sab divas saas. Naa badhan ghatan til saar" p-254. There are three more companions in the subtle body which always accompany the mind: Dharam Raj, Chitar Gupt, and Jumdoot. Dharam Raj is the Spiritual Judge of actions and thoughts of the mind which it experienced during its stay in the body, "Nanak jee upaaay kay likh naavay dharam bhaliaa" p-463, "Dharam Rai noon hukam hai baih sachaa dharam beechaar. Doojay bha-ay dusht-aatmaa oh teri sarkar" p-38. Chitar Gupt is the record keeper who watches over each thought of the mind during each breath and records it; it sorts out in which mode the breath was taken and presents a complete report to Dharam Raj: "Gaavay Chit Gupt likh jaanay, Likh likh dharam beecharay." At the end of the last breath of life, Jumdoot, the messenger of death, pulls the subtle body out of the physical body after breaking the knot. It arrests the mind and brings it to Dharam Raj for judgment based on the report submitted by Chitar Gupt. For a Gurmukh however, Chitar Gupt's report is destroyed and Jumdoot cannot touch them: "Chitar Gupt kagad faariaa jumdootan kachoo na chaalee" p-79. The report for the manmukh is analyzed and presented to God for writing the destiny, lekh for the next life: "Sabhna daa dar lekha hovay" p-952. These three subtle companions accompany the mind from its birth until it gets emancipated:

"Ja Tis bhaanaa taan jummian parvaar bhalaa paaiaa." p-921

Now to act in the world, the body is given five sensory organs: eyes to see, ears to hear, nose to smell, tongue to taste and the sense of touch to the hands and skin. With these senses the mind receives input and knows what is happening around it. Then there are five organs for doing 'karams' or actions: hands, feet, mouth, anus and genital organ. Thus, there are nine openings in the body through which mind goes out. There is a tenth invisible door called Tenth Door through which the mind enters its spiritual home called 'Nij Ghar': "Naun darvaaje kaaian kot hain dasvaan gupt rakheejaay" p-954. The tenth door is very hard and cannot be opened without the help of God's Sabad (Naam); "Bajar kapaat na khulni Gur Sabad khuleejay" p-954. The brain in the head serves to process the input from the mind from electronic messages through the nerves to the memory centers of the mind where the input is analyzed, recognized and action decided by the mind. This output is again converted as orders through the nerves of the brain and to the body which behaves according to the instructions of the mind. The brain is programmed to carry on the basic functioning of the body and tries to maintain good health in varying environmental conditions, interconnect the body and mind for safety of the body, and carry out the orders of the mind.

The body needs to be maintained in good health for the mind to carry out its duties. The body must be able to earn food and take care of itself while doing 'satvic' work such as sewa, Naam Japna, etc. Through this body, the mind has to connect with its spiritual source, God who also lives in it: "Ghat ghat mehn Harjoo bassay" p-427. Guru Ji calls the body a Temple of God: "Harmandar eh sareer hai" p-1346. It is only through this body that mind can connect with God: "Har ladha deh toleeay" p-927, "Vich kaaian nagar ladhaa Har bhalee" p-1134, "Tun mun khoj ghar meh paaia" p-1129, "Prabh abinasee ghar meh paaia" p-97. Those who search for the Divine Wealth outside of the body are fools and possessed by the demons of Maya: "Vin kaaiaa je hor thai Dhan khojde se moor betaalay" p-309.

We spoke earlier of the person who defines themself as their body. That person has a false ego of their mind and is controlled under Maya. However, everything belongs to God. The true mind is the child of God. Every thing in the universe belongs to God.

SURAT/CONSCIOUSNESS

Surat or consciousness is generally understood as a mental awareness about one's physical self, one's thoughts and what is happening around you. It helps one to analyze and act according to the decision one makes based on one's own intellect or in consultation with others for one's best interest. Surat relates to being awake and not the state of being asleep or in a coma.

In Gurbani, however, surat also relates to consciousness in dreams and a spiritually awakened state of mind when the mind is no longer captive of the five doots of Maya who were holding it spiritually asleep: "Mun soiaa maya bismaad" p-182. In this spiritually awakened condition, consciousness is merged with the Divine Consciousness and governs our thoughts, speech and action to be truthful; we become jeevan-mukat or liberated. The other state of consciousness is dreamless deep sleep. This state is called sunn in Gurbani. The mind in this state is thoughtless. This can be discussed in a separate missive. Let us now see what Gurbani mentions about consciousness.

This consciousness is given by the Creator God Himself to the mind, along with understanding and intellect and the mind perceives what God wants it to know:

"Surat matt chaturaee teri too janaay jaanaa Ram." p-779

The mind is the subtle manifestation of the Soul or Jot and it is its duty to realize this fact. God is always with the mind and it should make the best of this opportunity following the teachings of the Guru:

"Mun too jot saroop hain apnaa mool pahchaan.
Mun Har Ji teray naal hai gurmatee rang maan." p-441

Consciousness, understanding and intellect for the mind are shaped in Saram Khand (the zone of initiating development for mental beauty, such as a good or bad mental state):

"Tithay gharheeay surat matt mun budh." p-8

There is only one consciousness among all live beings created by God. None has been created without it:

"Eka surat jetay hain jeea. Surat vihoona koee na keea." p-24

God Himself awards honor and consciousness. Gurmukhs, the God-realized beings, are blessed by Him with glorious greatness:

"Sobha surat deh Prabh aap aapay gurmukh deh vadaaee." p-32

God Himself is the Sabad, His utterance, and consciousness is hearing the humming of the Sabad. He Himself observes and enjoys it all:

"Har aapay sabad surat dhun aapay.
Har aapay vekhay vigsay aapay." p-165

Sabad, the God's utterance, is true and God is telling the truth. His Consciousness is also true and He hears His true glories (as uttered by His devotees):

"Sabad sat sat Prabh bakta.
Sat sat sat jus sunta." p-285

Persons who are imbued with Sabad, God's utterance, are honored in the Court of the Lord. Consciousness of the Gurmukh is merge with the Supreme Consciousness. How can a faithless cynic, manmukh, or worshipper of energy attain enlightened consciousness through Sabad?

"Sakat nar sabad surat kion paaeeay." p-1042

Without awareness of Sabad one comes and goes in reincarnation:

"Sabad surat bin aeeay jaaeeay." p-1042

Understanding my own soul I have achieved the supreme state of consciousness which is now immersed in the service of the Lord:

"Atam cheen param pud paaiaa sewaa surat smaaee hay." p-1070

Awareness of Sabad within me I have started relishing the stirred ambrosial nectar:

"Surat sabad ridh antar jagee amio jhol jhol peejay ray." p-1074

Reading and studying they argue and debate. Attached to maya (of the three gunas) they waste their awareness to it:

"Parh parh loojhay baad vkhaanay mil maya surat gwaaee." p-1130

The surat attains spiritual awareness and wells up with faith of Naam through Naam Simran:

"Naa-ay maneeay surat upjay naamay mut hoee." p-1242

Without the Guru there is no spiritual awareness or achievement. Without the Guru there is no liberation:

"Gur bin surat na sidh Guru bin mukat na paa-vay." p-1399

Manmukhs are like ignorant childred or old men. They have no awareness of God within:

"Manmukh balak birdh smaan jinaa antar Har surat naheen." p-1399

The Gurmukhs never grow old (unlike the manmukhs) as they have spiritual awareness and wisdom in their consciousness:

"Gurmukh budhay kadee naheen jina antar surat gian." p-1418

It is very obvious from the above that consciousness belongs to God who awards it to all the live beings He creates. Life is with this surat and self realization is also with this surat. Illumination is obtained when it is connected to Sabad or Naam or the Soul within and finally merges with the Divine Consciousness. God Himself is Sabad, or Soul, and He Himself hears His own Sabad and watches His own created show:

"Apna khel Aap kar dekhay Thakur rachan rachaaiaa." p-272

There is nothing in this universe but God Himself in His own created nature in which He Himself sits, acts, observes and enjoys. The Soul is part of Himself; our mind is an extension of the Soul to deal with the physical world so it can play the part God assigned to us to play. It is God everywhere:

"Sabh Gobind Sabh Gobind hai Gobind bin naheen koee." p-1099

Praying for all of us for Gurkirpaa to connect us to Sabad, hence to Naam and then to our Mool-Supreme Consciousness.

NAAM JAPNA

Naam Japna is the first of the three basic duties of a Sikh; the other two are Kirat Karni and Wand Shakna. Naam Japna relates to the practice of remembering our Creator God and is done by repetitive utterance of God's Name which is given to us by our Guru Ji. The Name for remembering God given to us by Guru Ji is WAHEGURU. In simple English its meaning is 'Hail the Lord'. This is called Gur Mantra or the word to connect with God. Uttering Waheguru is praising God and the way it is practiced is singing His praises.

Repetition of this Name especially in Sat Sangat with devotion and respectful fear (bhau) creates love (bhaao) for God in our mind as it relates to our desire to unite with Him: "Nanak jin mun bhau tina mun bhaao." p-365. Naam Japna is not the end but a means to connect our consciousness with Naam which lies inside us: "Nau nidh amrit Prabh ka Naam. Dehi meh is kaa bisraam" p-293. Naam Japna is repeating the name in a cyclical manner, along with the breathing cycle (saas graas and saas saas as mentioned in Gurbani), and listening to it with full attention: "Ik chit ik mun dhiaa-ay" p-413. This takes our surti inside or disconnects it from the input of the five senses. In this condition, the mind is said to have gone into 'sunn' or a thoughtless state. The mind is disconnected from Maya and has gone where Naam/Sabad/Soul and God lives:

"Sargun Nirgun Nirankar sunn samadhi aap." p-390
"Sun smadh gufa teh aasan.

Kewal Brahm pooran teh basan." p-894

The regular practice of going into sunn where Naam is, starts cleaning the mind of dirt from Maya/'koor di paal':

"Oh dhopay Naavay kay rung." p-4

Soon one will start hearing Anhad Sabad from the outside. Anhad Sabad is the nonstruck Divine Melody which is non-stop in the Universe since the beginning, when God first uttered it to create the world: "Ek kwaao tay sabh hoaa" p-1003. A stage comes in Japna when one can hear the Anhad Sabad in sunn. This is called Amritsar in Gurbani: "Amrit eko Sabad hai Nanak Gurmukh paaia" p-644, and the mind bathes in it and cleanses itself of the dirt of Mayan thoughts and keeps becoming purer: "Mun dhovo Sabad laago Har sio raho chit laa-ay" p-1413. When the Sabad is heard in sunn Guru Ji advises us to pay full attention to it. Progressing towards Anhad Sabad will be followed by Sehaj Dhun, Toor and then Naad, which will take the mind to Sehaj Ghar: "Gur kahiaa sa kaar kamaao Sabad cheen Sehaj Ghar aa-ao" p-832. One has to pay attention to the Dhun of the Sabad heard inside of Sunn. Listening to this dhun will lead to self and God realization:

"Dhun meh dhiaan dhiaan meh jaania." p-879

It is our intellectual and scientific approach to interpret Gurbani which is causing us to misinterpret it. Gurbani is guiding us to connect with our true spiritual self which is not visible. That spiritual self is sitting inside us and cannot be observed by our five senses, which can deal only with physical input, whereas this spiritual phenomenon is taking place in sunn. The mind, a subtle being, is a child of God and is invisible like his father. No book of science or intellectual approach can help us here. Only Gurbani can guide us and a True Saint can show the technique or Vidhi for doing this.

The biggest hindrance in understanding Gurbani is interpreting Sabad as Gurbani. Sabad in the old Punjabi language means a sound and not the written word. When Guru Nanak Ji says "Sabad Guru surat dhun chela", he is not referring to his own uttered Gurbani, but the sound of the Divine utterance which one hears on an elevated spiritual path. Sabad is the utterance or communication of God with His creation through His Naam/Soul. This Sabad is going on in all of His creation as stated by Bhagat Naam Dev Ji: "Sabhe ghat Raam bole." This is the Sabad we have to connect to and follow to its source, our Creator Himself. Gurbani is advising us to connect to His Sabad. It is this Sabad which creates and destroys the creations and starts creation again:

"Utpat parlo Sabde hovay.
Sabde he phir opat hovay." p-117

Even Gurbani came to Gurmukhs (Gurus and Bhagats) through His Sabad and then they spoke it to us:

"Sabde upjay amrit Banee Gurmukh aakh sunvania." p-125

The life within us is this Sabad and it is this Sabad which connects us with our Husband God:

"Jeean andar jeeo Sabad hai jit Sauh milaava hoay." p-1250

It is through Sabad that we are connected to Naam and then through this Sabad (Toor and Naad) only that we connect with our Nirankar:

"Sabde he Naaon upjay Sabde mail milaaia." p-644

Sabad is our Guru and spiritual guide; Sabad is profound and unfathomable and without it the world is insane (ignorant of reality):

"Sabad Gurpeera gahar gambheera bin Sabde jag bauraanaa." p-635

This Sabad has been roaring in the universe for all the four yugs and O Audhoo, the Bhagats (spiritually awakened) have been listening to the message (banee) of the Sabad:

"Sabad soor jug chaaray Audhoo banee bhagat beechaaree." p-908

The Sabad dwells deep in the core of all beings and I see Invisible Supreme Being everywhere: "So Sabad kau nirantar vaasa alakh jaih dekhaan tah soee." p-944

Sabad veechar in Gurbani means to listen to Sabad and Sabad cheen means to recognize Sabad. This is one more instance where Sabad veechar is misunderstood as intellectual contemplation on Gurbani. The error is thus multiplied and completely throws us off the true meaning of it.

It is not my theory or concept, but when one reads Gurbani with this complete and correct understanding it will make it more meaningful and lots of confusion will go away. The Sabad Guru is alive and resides within each one of us and speaks to us: "Satgur mera sada sada na aa-vay na ja-ay. Oh abinasee Purakh hai jo sabh meh rahiaa smaa-ay" p-789. But it is us who have not opened our inner ears to it. No wonder Guru Ji calls us deaf and blind and our life a waste not having heard our Gur Pita:

"Sabad naa jaanay se unnhay bolay se kit aa-ay sansaaraa." p-601

Had I not ever actually heard Sabad myself, I would never be writing about Sabad in this way and I would continue the common understanding and mistranslations. Gurbani then made all the more sense to me. Again, the Gian, spiritual knowledge, started pouring down into you when you hear the Sabad and Gurbani writes about it:

"Giaan anjan Gur deea agiaan andher binaas." p-293
"Giaan dhiaan sabh Gur te hoee." p-831

To hear the Sabad, utterance of our Creator, Guru Ji recommends that we should find Sat Sangat and where they do Japna/Simrna and some have already advanced on this path. You will find out how to do Japna and Simran. Gurbani gives us three ways: Sas Graas, Saas Saas and Roam Roam. These three ways are applicable to different stages of Japna/Simrna. One will need guidance in this most misunderstood and difficult path. One needs the blessings of the Guru within and good karmas of past lives to get into it. When you are on the path, you need guidance of a True Sadh/Sant/Bhagat/ Brahmgiani to guide you in this territory of 'bikham marag', or difficult path. These individuals have gone over this difficult path and thus fully understand the hurdles and how to move you further along. Fake Sants have nothing to offer here and, instead, steal your money and your honor. The union comes only with the Grace of Waheguru (Gur Parsad). The path is very briefly described in the Four Laavan given at the end of this book.

It is very critical to know the Jugti, or technique, which the people higher on this path will explain. Our munmutt, which stands in the way, is a very challenging thing to give up and Guru Ji advises us to do Naam Japna everyday and get Gurmat from Guru within when you are connected with Him inside:

"Mun kee mutt tiaago Harjan eha baat kthainee.
Andin Har Har Naam dhiaavo Gur Satgur kee mutt lainee." p-880

Guru Ji mentions below about the need of Jugat:

"Sach ta par jaaneeay je jugat jaanay jeeo." p-466
"Nanak Satgur bhaiteeay poori hovay jugat." p-522

True saints carry the key to the house of wealth of Anhad Sabad:

"Anhad banee poonji.
Santan hath rakhee koonji." p-893

No intellectual short cut is on this path; one has to completely surrender oneself to the Guru (who resides within Sunn) and do as Gurbani and the Satguru inside guides you. Trust Him. He will guide you further on this path. Bhagti is Naam Japna but we have to acquire good qualities by being truthful in our thoughts, words and deeds to do bhagti:

"Vin gun keetay bhagat na hoay." p-4

Acquiring good qualities and being a good human is only the preparation to move speedily on the path of our bhagti to unite with our Creator. There is no exception to it unless God Himself out of His mercy and grace does it for someone and he/she better be deserving that out of their good past deeds.

It was only Guru Nanak who explained this path to the world and wrote it. He made it our duty to follow it while also doing truthful deeds to fulfill our Dharma as a human:

"Sarab dharam meh shresht dharam.
Har ka Naam Jap nirmal karam." p-266

METHODS IN NAAM JAPNA

To do Naam Japna, one needs to have a serious, intense desire and love for achieving higher spiritual states leading to union with God. To do so, one has to be truthful and honest in one's thoughts, words and deeds; "Vin gun kitey bhagat na hoey" p-4. The best time to practice Naam Japna is the early morning, 'amrit vela'. One should sit down cross legged on the floor or in any comfortable position so that body does not bother you. Gurmantra should be repeated with each breath loud enough so that you can hear it. You should have full attention on the sound of the mantra and you should not think of anything else: "Dhun mehn dhian, dhian mehn janian" p-879. Repeating the mantra while it is linked with breathing will form a 'dhun' or a tune you must listen to very attentively. To stop the mind from running around you have to make it busy with the dhun. There are three ways to do it:

Two point method (Saas Grass)

While breathing in you must say "Wah", listen to the sound and bring your attention to the tongue. While exhaling you must say "Guru" and bring your attention to the mool-duaar (1" below the naval point and 1" inside the stomach). Pay full attention to the sound of the word while inhaling and exhaling. Pull in your stomach a little bit while inhaling and let it go while exhaling. You should do the same in the other two methods. This will exercise your stomach while doing japna. You have to keep repeating this for at least an hour. It is difficult to say "wah" while inhaling but with some practice it will become easier.

You are cutting out the outside noises by speaking the mantra loudly and listening to it. At the same time you are keeping the mind engaged so it does not go astray by going up and down the points at your command. Depending on the intensity of your desire, your previous practice and the company of others joining with you in japna, your mind can come inside the body within weeks. It is not difficult. If you have the company of some gurmukhs who are already skilled at the process, it will take much less time and they will keep guiding you along the way.

Two point method (Saas Saas)

Sitting in the posture mentioned above, take a long breath in comfortably and while exhaling say "waheguru" slowly. Again start breathing in and start breathing out while repeating the mantra. Continue this process for one hour or more if time allows.

Four point method (Saas Sass)

This method is the same as 'saas saas' mentioned above but it is done slower, breaking up the mantra into four steps. Take a deep breath and chant "Wa", with your attention to the tongue listening attentively to the word (Wa). Then chant "Hey", bringing your attention to the heart level with full attention of the sound of the word (Hey). Then chant "Gu" with your attention to the naval point listening attentively to the sound of word (Gu). Then chant "Ru" bringing your attention to 'dharan' or 'mool duaar' (an inch below the naval point and an inch inside the stomach) paying full attention to the sound of the word (Ru). You have to start with word "Wa" and end with word "Ru" in the same breath while exhaling. Then take a full breath and repeat. This method helps to bring the mind home faster and is generally done before the two point method. Gradually tone down the voice to silence and just listen to the gurmantra in your mind. When we become adept in this method, only go to the next method.

Rom-Rom method

Sit comfortably and feel your pulse on the left wrist with the fingers of your right hand. Recognize the rhythmic sound of your heart beat, 'lub-dub' rhythm. This method is not restricted to breathing. Take a deep breath, hold it for a second, chant 'Wahe- Guru' internally without making a sound, and synchronize it with lub-dub of your heart beat. A daily practice of this routine eventually causes every cell in the body to vibrate and resonate with the sound current of 'Wahe-Guru' synchronized with your heart beat. Gradually, everything you come in contact with will seem to be chanting 'Waheguru,' Waheguru' in a spontaneous and continuous stream, a divine sound. This method of simran is called 'rom-rom' simran:

"Gurmukh rom rom Har dhiavai." p-941

This method should be tried only after mastering the other three methods and under the guidance of a master.

Japna and Sunn State

After some practice, the body will first go into smadhi and then the mind will go into sunn. When the mind goes into sunn, you will not be conscious of your surroundings or any noise around you. Your neck will limp down as if you are asleep, but you will not dream or think. The moment any thought comes into your mind you will be awake, very relaxed, calm and serene. That effect may last for hours or the whole day. It will be a very pleasant and energizing feeling and you would like to go back into it again.

Even before achieving the sunn state, you may have started hearing anhad sound in your ears like that of flute, drums, chirping birds, rebaab, heartbeat, dancing bells, etc. Don't be surprised or think that something has gone wrong with your ears. Your ears are now attuned to hearing anhad sabads. Try focus on listening to these sounds; it will help you in performing japna better.

There are four levels of loudness of japna:

1. Baikhri - loud enough for you and others to hear around you.
2. Madhmaa - Only you can hear it.
3. Pasanti - Saying it inside your mind. You can hear it within.
4. Pra - You don't recite japna. You can hear it inside while in sunn.

Don't be embarrassed about saying the gurmantra loud, this is the fastest way to break your mind into simran and away from the thoughts of Maya. Japna should start with 'Baikhri,' then it goes into 'Madhmaa' and finally into 'Pasanti'. 'Pra' japna happens in sunn and is without you doing it, but you can hear it. Japna in 'Baikhri', 'Madhmaa' and 'Pasanti' is equivalent to beating the mind to straighten it out. Guru Ji says, "If you have to beat, beat the mind. By doing so you get it away from 'Jum', the demon of death:

"Kootan so jo mun ko kootey, mun kootey to jum te chootey." p-872

People don't understand why you are saying gurmantra so loud and will not like it, but please don't pay any attention to it:

"Jion jion Raam kahe jun oochey, nar nindak dunss lagaaee." p-872

Your Japna to a munmukh will be like a snake bite. There is much more to it but I think this will be good enough to start. It can be explained better in a personal meeting with a teacher. All I have written is based on personal experience and guidance from SGGS and Gurmukhs. This is the only way to go into sunn and have a vision of the mind and, later, a vision of God. You have got to have lot of love for God.

SUNN

Sunn is the state of consciousness where the mind is thoughtless. The mind goes through four stages of sunn before it is awakened from its sleep under 'mayan' thoughts. This state of mind is called Turiya Awasthaa, Chautha Pud or Param Pud. At this state of human mind one rises above virtues and vices and can meet and merge with the Consciousness of the Supreme Being. Within our body and outside it there are three worlds of sunn; on earth, above earth and below earth. But the human mind is always absorbed in thoughts. To quiet the mind it needs the help of Naam Japna, which breaks the mind's link with breathing. Then its consciousness goes inside the body into the sunn zone where it becomes thoughtless. This is the first state of the mind in sunn.

Next the mind merges with the air in the ambience of the sunn state within the body. This is the second state of sunn. The next stage in the process is where the mind starts hearing anhad sabad in the sunn state. This is called the third stage of the mind in sunn. With these sabads, Naam starts cleansing the mind of its filth of Maya. When it hears sehaj dhun it has then reached the tenth door just outside the Sach Ghar or Divine Mansion waiting for the Grace of God or Gurparsaad. When that happens, it hears Naad, sheds the air and is welcomed into Nij Ghar and Sach Ghar with sounds of the Panch Sabad: "Vaajay panch sabad titt ghar subhagay." Here the mind is completely rid of Maya and is back into its pure spiritual state. The mind is fully awakened to its spiritual reality and has become gurmukh/jiwan mukat or where the mayan forces are dead while the body is still alive or above virtues and vices. The mind at this stage has reached the fourth stage in sunn:

"Antar sunnum bahar sunnum treebhavan sun msunum.
Chauthee sunnay jo nar jannay tisko paap na punnum." p-943

This is the house of the True One as told by the Satguru and is also the true house of His child, our mind (who is on a physical journey on this planet, Earth):

"Satgur tay paa-ay veechara.
Sunn Samadh Sachay Ghar baraa." p-1037

This is the state of pure consciousness of the mind, the child of God, when it merges with the Supreme Consciousness of The Creator God. This is the state He is always in, a state of sunn smadh. God does not come out of this state unlike a gurmukh who has to come out of it into the three gunas to carry out his worldly responsibilities. If one has neither experienced sunn nor a spiritually awakened mind, it will not be intellectually possible to comprehend this state.

God operates only through this deep sunn state and has the spiritual powers to create anything He thinks. His Word/Sabad/Naam carries the power. These powers are defined in Gurbani as 'ridh'and 'sidh'. Gurmukhs get it too but they do not use it for any selfish reason or to show off their powers. All Gurus had it and they used it wherever they were permitted to do so in obedience to God's Hukam. It does not matter whether scientists or rational people accept it or not.

We can keep on discussing what sunn is and from where this continuous sunn came into being. Who are those attuned to this sunn? Guru Ji answers that they are like the Lord, Who created these powers in them:

"Sunno sunn khay sabh koee.
Anhat sunn khaan tay hoee.

Anhat sunn rattay se kaisay.

Jistay upjay tis hee jaisay." p-943

In the sunn the Infinite Lord assumes Power. He Himself is unattached, infinite and incomprehensible. He Himself creates and beholds His creation and produces more sunn. Air and water were created from sunn. He produced the world and bodies for minds, their ruler:

"Sunn kala aprampar dharee.
Aap niraalam apar apaaree.
Aapay kudrat kar kar dekhay sunno sunn upaa-inda.
Pavan panee sunnay tay saajay.
Shrisht upaa-ay kaanian garh raajay." p-1037

I have no idea what mathematical equation we can apply to creation by the Almighty Creator when there is nothing material on one side but everything in the infinite universe on the other side. His powers are beyond our comprehension. He is the Divine Consciousness, Divine Power, Divine Wisdom, Divine Intelligence, Divine Order, His Utterance lives forever, He supports His Creation sitting within it, He runs His Play in His infinite Universe, He is the single Spectator, He is the Actor, Director, Producer and Observer of His Play. He can Create and Destroy as it pleases Him. He is afraid of none, depends on none and loves His Creation.

He is hungry for praise just like us:

"Har Ji apnee vadiaee bhavdee." p-652

He is hungry for our love and devotion:

"Gobind bhaao bhagat da bhukhaa." - Bhaee Gurdaas

He is ready to give the whole world for love:

"Fareeda jay too meraa hoay rahen sabh jag tera hoay." p-1282

A Bhagat can override His decision but He doesn't do that to Bhagat's:

"Meri bandhee Bhagat shdaa-ay bandhay Bhagat naa shootay mohay." p-1252

If God is all that, can we just call Him energy when He is everything and even us? Are we willing to call ourselves energy? Can we, the tiny creatures on this infinitesimally small planet judge the Infinite One and put an equation on Him? If we do not know who we are, can we judge the Infinite Lord of this infinite creation?

I end with prayers to Guru Ji for his blessings on us for Bibek Budhi.

SUNN — SOME QUESTIONS

There are many a question by those who are curious about sunn, have some experiences with it, and others who are on their way to it and have made some progress in naam simran or sunn. Let me make some comments on sunn on the basis of what is written in Gurbani, personal experience and that of other Gurmukhs:

1. Sunn is a very common condition of the mind which all of us experience during sleep. When the body initially goes into sleep there will be body jerks when the mind lets go of the body. After the mind releases its hold on the sense organs, it goes into a dream mode thinking of trai-bhavan (the air, earth and sky). Maya dwells there with the three gunas and the mind enters into a deep sleep (dreamless state) which is the same as sunn of the mind; it may last for a short while. It is during this time the mind makes its contact with its creator God, who gives the hungry mind some dose of naam. This dose keeps the mind's sanity as it may not earn that by naam japna. Here, the next day's plan is told to the mind. As the mind does not know God, it does not recognize Him but acts on the plan thinking that it is his plan. This is how God acts as 'daaia' for the mind at night. So sunn is no yoga or anything special which we do. Do not be scared or confused as you go through sunn every night.

2. God lives in sunn and our mind is the child of God sent to this world to play its role in God's drama, which is played here. To meet Him, the mind must go into sunn; "Sargun nirgun Nirankar sunn smaadhee Aap" p-290. During naam-simran, focusing on

the dhun of the gurmantar sends the mind into the body by letting the sense organs go. The body goes into smadhi while the mind goes into sunn, thereby it is not thinking. The mind in this state is said to have gone into sunn which is equivalent to a dreamless state. You are then in the zone of naam which acts on the mind by cleaning it; slowly the mind starts hearing the sabad inside. The cleansing of the mind makes it purer and purer so it is able to hear other sabads and finally obtains naam.

3. The mind is pure enough to see God, when the mind sees naam or the bright light, and when God by its grace or gurparsaad removes whatever ego the mind has: "Haumay sabad jlaa-ay" p-458. The mind sees nothing but the light of God in the Fourth sunn and the mind becomes just like God Himself: "Jistay upjay Tis Hee jaisay" p-843. The mind is then in turiya awasthaa or param/chauthaa pud. The mind in that state is fully awakened by naad: "Dhun upji sabad jgaaia" p-1039. The mind is enlightened with the Jot of God and can see everything even with its eyes closed in sunn: "Akhee bajho vekhnaan vin kanee sun-nan" p-139. At this stage one is supposed to have acquired 'drib drishtee'. Even with the eyes opened, one can see the halo of God within, the presence of God in other people, and the presence of God in everything else. In this state 'naam rus' or naam varkha goes on in the body when mind is focused on it.

4. There are other conditions of the body and mind that are experienced by some people when given the grace of God. The body can go into smadhi mode but the mind has not yet let the vision go. The body is trying to go into smadhi but mind is not letting it go because it is attached to the senses. That is partial smadhi. More effort is required to go into full smadhi.

5. One can use different techniques of reaching God/Naam by focusing on the air or breaths and connecting with naam as air is the first child of God/ Naam: "Saachay tay pavna bhaiaa" p-151. But in such cases one will get Naam Nectar/rus only so long as they are in touch with Naam. They gain a lot of knowledge as they are in touch with Satguru. If they get turiya awasthaa they will not retain it till they go into sunn. But it is a fairly advanced stage.

6. Till one has experienced the state of sunn and higher states in sunn one will neither believe in it nor will they interpret Gurbani correctly. Guru Ji is describing the actual path that the teacher called gur-poora (who has gone through all this). I wish them good luck. This is a spiritual path and not an intellectual path. One learns it only after traveling on it. Intellect/logic is of no help in this area:

"Mun baichay satgur kay paas.
Tis sevak kay karaj raas." p-1258

I wish all a very happy journey to nij-ghar/thir ghar which is our own spiritual home. Please keep trying. Guru Ji is only waiting for you to see us there. Get rid of the five doots of maya who are holding us back.

The location of our real spiritual home is Nij Ghar. It can be reached from within our body by silencing the mind and traveling inwards with the help of Sabad Guru, Anhad Banee, Toor and Naad. The door opens by Gurparsaad when our Father, Parmaatmaa Himself, receives and greets us back home after our arduous journey through the Country of Kaal in Bhavjal Sagar, where we remained lost for four ages. Our very kind Satguru makes it accessible for us. How very lucky we are to have a True Guru in Sri Guru Granth Sahib, who helps us obtain our bliss, the 'anand,' back to us permanently.

OUR NIJ GHAR – THE FOURTH SUNN

Our mind thinks incessantly and does not hold still even for an instant. Under all sorts of distractions it wanders aimlessly in all directions. Only with good fortune can someone find a perfect Guru, who gives the mantra of the Lord's Name that makes the mind quiet and tranquil after Naam Japna:

"Eh mun na tikay bauhrangee deh dis dhavay.
Gur poora paaia vadbhagee Har Mantar deea mun thadhay." p-171

Naam Japna does this to a wandering mind. It tries to make the mind still till it stops thinking. It is then lured into the 'dhun' of the japna and the mind comes inside where it is totally disconnected from the input of the five sense organs. The mind becomes totally thoughtless, a condition called 'sunn' in Gurbani. In this condition, the mind stops giving any instructions to the body, which becomes still and is said to be in 'smadhee'.

It is in this condition the mind is disconnected from the world of Maya of the three modes and comes into the body where Naam/ Sabad is present. This space where the mind comes into is called 'sunn mandal'. Gurbani mentions sunn many a time, as the location of Naam, Satguru and God. The purpose of Naam Japna is to disconnect the mind from Maya and its bad effects in Raj Gun and Tum Gun so it can be cleaned with Naam/Sabad: "Bhareeay matt papaan kay sung. O dhopay naavay kay rung." Sabad is God's utterance in all the bodies: "Ghat ghat vaajay naad" and cleans the dirt caused by Mayan thoughts:

"Mun dhovo sabad laago Har sio raho chit laa-ay." p-919

The inner journey for spiritual development is through sunn where Naam/Sabad Guru (which is also called Satguru in Gurbani) resides. Satguru not only gives spiritual knowledge but also prepares the mind for meeting with Nirankar:

"Sabade he Naaon upjay sabade mail milaaia." p-646

When the mind initially enters sunn, it is said to be sitting in the FIRST SUNN. When the thoughtless mind in sunn merges with the ambience of the sunn mandal it adopts the nature of the air there, the first creation of God/Sach:

"Saachay te pavna bhaiaa." p-19
"Suneh sunn miliaa samdarsi pavan roop ho jaae-geh." p-1103

This condition of mind in Sunn Mandal when it merges with the air is called the SECOND SUNN.

As the journey in sunn progresses, Anhad Sabad, the unstruck divine melodies, are heard in the second sunn. These are the utterances of the Nirankar inside us as Sabad Guru. It is here that mind begins to be cleansed by Sabad/Naam to prepare for the journey to the goal. This zone in the sunn mandal is called Amritsar, or Pool of Ambrosial Nectar of Naam, where the mind bathes in to clean itself:

"Antar koohnta Amrit bharia." p-570

Devtas, or angels (non-visible bodies, which were once in human form), live in the zone called Dev Sathan where the three gunas are also present. It is a zone after physical death as they did not reach Nirankar yet:

"Dev sathanay kia nissani.
Taih baajay Sabad anahad banee." p-974

Devtas are stuck here and cannot go beyond it because they did not do
enough bhagti to cross over the 'bhavjal sagar'. They don't have to be
born again, but can't go beyond Dev Sathan to unite with Nirankar.
They beg God to give them another chance in the human body so that
they can do more bhagti to crossover to the higher level:

"Is dehi ko simray dev.
So dehee bhaj Har kee sev." p-1159

The mind surrounded by Anhad Sabad is called the THIRD SUNN.
This is also called 'dhaval', a cross over between Bhavjal Sagar and
Nij Ghar. Here the mind is with the air and it sheds it before entering
the next sunn. This location is also called 'dar' or doorway to the
Sach Mehal/Parkash Mehal/Mansion of the Divine. It is this state
that Guru Nanak Ji is writing about in 27th Pauri of Jap Ji Sahib. He
describes the symphony of celestial music going on at the gate of
the Sach Ghar where all of God's creation is singing praises to Him:

"So dar keha so ghar keha jit beh sarab smaalay.
Vaajay naad anake asankha ketay vavanhaary.
Ketay raag paree sio kaheean ketay gavanharay.
Gaavay tohnau paun panee baisantar gavay raja dharan duaaray." p-6

The next step in the path comes when the mind is fully cleansed of
the filth of Maya and is waiting for the Grace of God to open the
Tenth Door to let His child in. This is preceded by the sounds of
Toor and Naad:

"Anhad Banee Naad vajaaia." p-375

The Tenth Door opens amidst the sounds of the Five Sabads. The
mind is welcomed home having conquered the five doots of Maya.

The mind sheds the air and is illumined with the Jot of God and is fully awakened to its spiritual self by the Sabad:

"Dhun upjee Sabad jgaai." p-1039

Free from the bondage of Maya, the mind sees nothing but Parkash or Divine Light/Jot and finally meets the Beloved Lord:

"Pargati Jot milay Ram Piaray." p-375

This happens with the Grace of the Guru that one meets the Lord and finds perfect peace and tranquility with such ease:

"Guru Nanak tutha miliaa Har Raaia.
Sukh raen vihaani sehaj subhaaia." p-375

The Perfect Lord, Brahm, dwells in sunn-smadh in this area and holds discussions with Bhagats. There is no happiness or grief, nor death or birth (but absolute tranquility):

"Sunn samadh gufa te asan.
Kewal Brahm pooran teh basan.
Bhagat sung Prabh gosht karat.
Taha harakh naa soag naa janam marat." p-894

This is the Fourth SUNN and the end of the mind's journey back to its Nij Ghar and Sehaj Ghar. Here, it can live in perfect bliss and becomes Jiwan Mukat, liberated while alive.

This sunn is also called Anhad Sunn. Those minds who reach this sunn become just like the One Who created them:

"Anahad sunn rattay se kaisay.
Jistay upjay tishee jaisay." p-943

Sunn prevails inside and outside of all the three zones; earth, sky and nether-lands. In the fourth sunn, the mind becomes Gurmukh, its karmas are over and is not judged for these:

"Antar sunan bahar sunnan tri-bhavan sunam sunan.
Chauthai sunun jo nar jaanai ta ko paap na punnan." p-943

This is the house of the True One as told by the Satguru and is also the true house of His child, the mind who is on a physical journey on this planet, Earth:

"Satgur tay paa-ay veechara.
Sunn Samadh Sachay Ghar bara." p-1037

Gurbani guides us in how to make it to our true home while alive and how to become a jeevan-mukat. At the end of our physical life we land straight into Nijh Ghar and are met with our Father, Nirankar, who greets us with a hug and congratulates us for our victory in the fight with the five doots of Maya:

"Jo jan Har Prabh Har Har sarna tin dargeh Har Har deh vadiaaee.
Dhan dhan sabaas kahay harjan ko Nanak mel la-ay gal laee." p-493

Gurmukhs thus establish an easy access route to Nij Ghar from Bhavjal Sagar via sunn, Anhad Sabad, Toor and Naad and they followed this route back for their mundane responsibilities:

"Gurmukh aavay jaa-ay nisang." p-932

REINCARNATION

We the human species and all others in the universe are given a body in which we live in for this world. It is given for a certain specified time and then this body stops to function, which is called death. The death is of the body in which the being lived. The being is originally enclosed in the invisible subtle body called 'sookham moorat.' When the being leaves the body, the mind in it is judged for its karmas done during its lifetime:

"Sookham moorat Naam Niranjan kaayaan ka akaar." p-466

The subtle body contains the soul, called immaculate Naam of God, and the mind is tied to the physical body at a point below the belly button called 'dharan' or 'mool duaaar':

"Mool duaray bandhia bandh." p-1159

At the time of death, when the body takes the last of the breaths allowed for the lifetime, "Gin ghalay sab divas saas, na badhan ghatan til saar" p-254, this knot is opened by the order of God: "Khullee ganth utho likhiaa aaiaa Ram" p-1110. The sookham is pulled out of the physical body by the messenger of death, 'jumdoot'. The mind is presented for judgment to 'Dharam Raj', who reports to God and judges all truthfully:

"Dharam Rai noon hukam hai beh sacha dharam bichaar." p-38

If not having achieved the goal of the life spent here on earth, the mind is given another body according to the divine judgment; it is born again to achieve salvation. This rebirth of the being enclosed in the 'sookham moorat' is called reincarnation. The being is allowed another chance for achieving 'moksha' in the human body or a lower physical form based upon its karmas in that life. If the being is born as any other species, its next birth will be the same, lower, or another higher physical form as it progresses further towards the human form. For it is only in the human form where the being's ultimate union with God can occur. We will discuss here the human life only as the Sri Guru Granth Sahib elaborates.

The goal of human life is to achieve union of the soul with the Creator God from whom it was separated from at the time of the first incarnation. The body is given to the mind for doing its karmas during its time allotted. The mind, the child of God; "Kauh Kabir eh Ram ki uns" p-871 is the ruler of the body which Guru Ji calls its 'nagry' or town:

"Kayan nagry eh mun raja." p-907

It is the mind who performs all the deeds (karmas) good or bad. The mind is created by the five basic components, 'tutts', from its original spiritual state due to entanglement in maya of the three gunas:

"Eh mun karma eh mun dharma eh mun panch tutt te janma." p-415

The soul, which is part of God, makes the body, gives it life, and also advises and guides the mind to do the right things. It is the soul which is separated from God and wants to go back to God. It calls upon the mind to come home (within the body) so that it can meet with Har Guru, the Creator Lord who also resides in the body:

"Mere mun pardesi vay piaaray aao ghare.
Har Guru milaavo meray piaarey Har vassay gharay." p-951

The soul's union with God is its salvation for which the mind has to work towards. The mind must draw its attention from the outside to the inside with the help of Naam Japna, which allows its surti or consciousness to come in. The mind's thoughts, which were polluted by Maya, are cleansed by Naam which is the soul itself:

"Bhareeay mutt papan ke sung.
Oh dhopay Naave ke rung." p-4

Once the mind is fully cleansed, it sees the Light of Naam and realizes its spiritual nature. The mind has to work harder to stay in enlightenment even longer till it breaks away its entanglements with Maya. With God's Grace it becomes qualified to go into its spiritual home, which Guru Ji calls Nij Ghar; it then achieves salvation or mukti. The mind and soul do not have to be reincarnated into another body to complete any more karma. That is because its karmas have ended and the mind and soul are reunited with its Father, God. The mind and soul then live in bliss, which was what it was looking for in the physical world of Maya, run by Kaal. All of this is happening as it is participating in the cosmic play of God, who started it and is enjoying His own creation:

"Apna khel aap kar dekhe
Thakur rachan rachaaiaa." p-292

He makes all humans different and unique to His liking and to fit as different characters in His play in this world:

"Meray Prabh Saachay ik khel rachayaa.
Koeey na kishee jehaa upaayaa." p-1056

It is God Himself who first creates us as per His plan to play different roles by enticing us to be captivated by Maya, who leads the whole world astray:

"Tudh aapai jagat upaaykay aappay dhanday laaiaa.

Moh thagaulee paaykay tudh apau jagat bhulaaiaa." p-138

We are not aware that we are mere actors playing different roles in His world theater in various forms, but basically remaining the same. He makes us wander through countless incarnations in doubts and never having dwelled in peace:

"Nattooaa bhekh dikhaavay bauh bidh jaisaa hai oh taisa re.
Anak joan bharmio bharam bheetar sukhay nahee parvesa re." p-403

We suffer playing those roles, go through pain and pleasures, and are tormented when we lose our physical belongings and members of our family, which we think are ours. We react to different things happening to us in life and this keeps His play going. We are afraid of death thinking that this is the end of life, whereas, it is just shedding of this body and getting another new one to keep his play going. The real self, the soul and mind, never die. We only come and go according to His Will and are immortal like our Creator:

"Eh to rachan rachyaa Kartar aavat jaavat hukam apaar." p-885
"Na ko mooa na marne joag nahee binse abnaasee hoag." p-885

We are not what we think we are and Guru Ji is all praise for those who know the reality:

"Jo eh deesay so eh naaheen jananhare kau bal bal jaao." p-885

God sent us Satguru to make us understand reality. Satguru explained to us His game and showed us the way out of the sufferings of life, fear, and death. The path is to cleanse the mind of its attachment to the 'koor' of Maya and then connect it to Naam, which he calls Guru/ Sabad Guru/Satgur. This process prepares the mind for its mokhsa, salvation. This gives it freedom into a blissful world, in the company of our Pure Creator who manifests everywhere as a Formless Being in a primal transcendent state of equipoise:

"Sargun Nirgun Nirankar sun samadhi aap." p-290

The only place we can meet Him is in the state of equipoise or sunn/ samadhi and we have to go there. Naam Japna takes our mind into that state and helps us further as explained above. But only rare ones ponder upon the Sabad/ Gurbani:

"Baani birlo bichaarsi je ko gurmukh hoay." p-935

God's play keeps going and we keep on playing our part in it. We continuously encounter happiness, grief, and blame our sufferings on others, while we ignore Guru Ji's advice written in the SGGS Ji. Here is what Guru Ji tells us about reincarnation. We are born and then we die and keep coming and going under His Will:

"Jamnaa marnaa hukam hai bhaanay aavay jaa-ay." p-742

Wandering and roaming through 8.4 million incarnations, we now have been given this priceless human body, which is so difficult to obtain:

"Lakh chaurasee bharmate bharmte dulabh janam ub paaiyo." p-101

Faithless cynics are bound to karmas and forced to wander in reincarnations. They die and are reborn and continue to come and go:

"Sakat moorhe bandh bhavaeey mar janme aaee jaee hai." p-1026

Without meditative remembrance on God, they come and go and are cast in the womb of hellish reincarnations:

"Bin simran aavay fun jaavay garabh joni narak majhara hai." p-1030

You have wandered through countless lives and have suffered through many incarnations. You have forgotten the True Lord and are bearing a lot of sufferings:

"Kot janam bharam aaiaa piaaray anak joan dukh paaiaa.
Sacha Sahib vissariaa piaaray bauhti mile sja-ay." p-640

Worshipping the One Lord in the company of the holy, the pain of birth and death are removed:

"Bhaj sang saadhu Ek araadho janam maran dukh naasay." p-691

The gurmukhs, spiritually enlightened persons, whose mind are absorbed in the remembrance of Hari, the God, will overcome the sufferings of reincarnations:

"Gurmukh Har Har Har liv laage janam maran do-ou dukh bhage." p-1178

Countless references are present about reincarnation in SGGS. They don't leave any doubt in one's mind about the validity of reincarnation. God's whole play is based on reincarnation. It is just like us when we run plays in theaters and make movies; we cast the same actors in different roles, as we play these roles in God's plays life after life. We eventually stop when God and Guru Ji's blessing is given to us which takes us out of this coming. We are connected with holy company where we bond with Sabad/Satguru/Naam. Finally, we are uniting with the True Lord and live in His blissful company along with the other lucky ones who are already there. Once there, we come to realize that it is nobody but God everywhere and in everyone:

"Sabh Gobind hai sabh Gobind hai Gobind bin nahee koee." p-485

WHY KNOW REINCARNATION

Reincarnation gives a perspective on this life that God has given us. Does life begin for us when we are born and acquire this body and does it end at death when we shed this body? This makes you think about whether we are the body or someone else who lives in the body. If this is the only life we have on this planet, what is the purpose of it?

Are we born just to live some years? The early part is dependent on our parents who prepare us for a vocation. Then we find a job or start a business to earn our living. Then we get married and raise some children. Then we take care of them and then die of old age, disease or an accident. That is what an ignorant man without any Guru will do. But what if we, as Sikhs, have a Guru who knows about the life and the purpose of it and tells us this?

Our Guru tells us that we are born in the human life after having lived through 8.4 million species. The purpose of this life is to unite with our Creator, God/Akal Purakh/Waheguru, while living a truthful life and doing bhagti on His Name. If this is the goal of life given to us, as humans can we fulfill it in one lifetime? Again, Guru Ji says only a rare one, among a million, remembers God in his heart. So what happens if we can't meet our goal at the end of life? Are we born again to meet the goal given to us? Are we born again to continue if we fail, as we do in our educational schools? God is kind enough to give us more chances to complete our mission in life. These new chances are called reincarnations. It has nothing to do with whether we are Sikh or belong to other religions. We are children of One God and all are treated the same way. Those who are guided by a True Guru know the right way and others do not. As participants in God's Play here, we go on as Sikhs or not.

Most of us do not care about the teachings of the Guru or gurmat and just follow other ignorant ones. Their goal in life is chasing happiness by acquiring wealth or fame, but in the end they die leaving everything behind. Guru Ji talks about such people in the seventh Pauri of Japji Sahib. A man, who is known in all the nine parts of this planet while the whole world praises him, will become a worm of worms and even criminals will call him a criminal if he did not care to meet the goal of life.

Then why God does not tell us about all this. Yes, He did it through the Gurus. The Gurus claim that this Gurbani is not theirs, but they are delivering a message from God Himself. It is unto us to believe in it or not. If we do believe, then they affirm reincarnation for those who have not become Gurmukhs or die as manmukhs. Many griefs are planned in the life of a manukh so that he falls into prayer to God for relief or is provided the company of true saints or Gurmukhs. In this company he is directed back to the mission. This happens when God's grace falls upon him.

Those who do not pay attention to Gurbani and are driven by their own limited mind, body, and intellect do not believe in it and misinterpret Gurbani to prove that they think they know better. They makes it look like Guru is wrong or was writing under the influence of other holy books, which means what the Guru wrote is not God's message.

Not knowing about reincarnation as a part of life indicates we do not know about life, its purpose, and God's Will by which we have to live. We assume we know what to do with life and make plans to achieve success per our own will. When these plans do not work out we become unhappy and sometimes miserable. Not believing in Gurbani, we keep on trying our own alternatives for happiness and nothing seems to work. We then do not know what else to do and may even commit suicide. Is that how our life should end, creating more misery for those dependent on us when Guru is there to help and advise us? In this situation, we are running our life without guidance from Guru or we are Guru-less, which we do not care to admit.

Some say, if we know about reincarnation we will become lazy and may not work hard enough to achieve our goals. It will be equivalent to not doing our homework while going to school. Are we not reprimanded for that, may fail the class, and suffer shame as a failed student? It is the same when we are asked about our mission in life. If we fail, we are treated roughly by the jumdoots whereas Gurmukhs are honored for having done well in life. Only the Guru tells us this in Gurbani. As a Gursikh, we are supposed to believe in Gurbani. Otherwise, what good Sikhs are we?

When we are born again why we do not remember the past life? The plan is for you not to remember it, to treat this life as a new gift from God, and to enjoy living it to the fullest extent. If we knew about our past failures and ill deeds we did, we will be very unhappy, guilty to face life, and may not be able to enjoy this life at all. As one of Nature's oddities, some children remember their past lives, but their parents do not understand them. The children feel ridiculed and say it no more so they can soon try to forget it. There are thousands of such cases documented in writing and in documentaries. Regression hypnosis can take you back into past lives and you can trace your own past and speak about it. This is recorded for you to listen.

The human life is a gift from God to us. The soul and mind are on their physical journey on this planet. It is worthwhile to know about this most valuable gift which God has given to us before we start playing with it and end up as failures in life. God sent us help for us to know about this life and its purpose by sending His messenger, Guru Nanak. He was here to inform and guide us to make the best of this opportunity to achieve bliss in life, avoid the recurrence of being born again, and going through failures and grief. It is up to us to make the best of it or we will die unhappy having lost a chance for bliss.

SPIRITUALITY

Spirituality is a state of mind being with its true self, the spirit within us, the atma/soul or Parmaatmaa/God who pervades the entire universe. This state can only be understood by experiencing it as it is beyond our intellectual comprehension because of our limited mind body intellect. Spirituality relates to infinite spirit which manifests the infinite creation of the Creator Lord who also created us for a role in His play on this blue planet Earth in this solar system. We have come to know a little bit about the Earth and the solar system and are only guessing about the rest of the infinite universe and putting up theories about its creation and end. But only the Creator knows about His universe and how He created it: "Ja Karta shrishti ko saajay aapay jaanay soee." p-4. Only those who tried to speak about His creation became one with the Creator but they also had no words to describe it and, therefore, say:

"Teri kudrat toon hai jaany aur na doojaa janay." p-1185

It is hard to describe the state of being spiritual in our language of the physical world as there are no words for it. Those who try to describe do repent it. Guru Ji calls it the state of acceptance or 'mannay':

"Mannay kee gatt kahee naa jaa-ay.
Jay ko k-hay pishay pashtaa-ay." p-3

Spirituality is the state of Gurmukhs who have achieved union with God and whose mind is pure and clear of the effects of Maya, or worldly thoughts of three gunas which are 'raj gun', 'tum gun' and 'sat gun'. The mind of a manmukh is always absorbed in these thoughts which keep it tied to the thoughts of the physical world called 'bhavjal sagar' of Yaya in Gurbani: "Raj gun tum gun sat gun kaheeay eh teri sabh maya" p-1123. The ones who have their mind set on achieving the fourth pud or stage achieve emancipation/salvation/moksh/sehaj or permanent bliss:

"Chauthay pud ko jo nar cheenay tin he param pud paya." p-1123

For achieving the fourth stage we are advised to avoid raj gun and tum gun and have to think and act in sat gun. Raj gun gives rise to plans and ambitions for achieving worldly success and fame whereas tum gun leads you into desires for lust, anger, greed, attachments and ego. Both raj gun and tum gun turn you away from your spiritual source, God. Whereas in sat- gun your thoughts and actions direct you to truthfulness, contentment, self discipline, compassion, virtuous living, service to others, meditation on the name of God, etc. This prepares the ground leading one towards spirituality. But the thoughts and actions in sat gun are not spirituality itself. Guru Ji advises us to renounce our cleverness and intellectual pride, which though difficult to do, by meditating on the name of God every day and thereby acquiring the spiritual wisdom of the Satguru:

"Mun kee matt tiaago har jan eha baat kathainee.
Andin Har Har Naam dhiaavo gur satgur kee mutt lainee." p-800

This happens when the surti or consciousness of the mind goes inside the body during naam japna/simrna and contacts the jewel of naam, the divine elixir within us: "Nau nidh amrit Prabh ka naam dehi meh is ka bisram" p-293. This cleanses the mind of the dirt of Mayan thoughts when it hears the anhad sabad, the divine melody going on non-stop within the body: "Sabhay ghat Ram bolay" p-698, in the sunn samadhi state: "Mun dhovo sabad laago Har sio raho chit laa-ay" p-919. It is the anhad sabad which one hears in sunn that takes one to sehaj ghar, the house of tranquility or bliss in the fourth state of the mind when one focuses its surti on these:

"Gur kahiaa saa kaar kmaavo.
Sabad cheen sehaj ghar aavo." p-832

It is sabad that brings out naam and connects the mind to Paramatma:

"Sabday he naaon upjay sabday mael milaaya." p-123

Spirituality evolves to different higher levels as mind goes through this journey towards the union with Paramaatmaa. This journey is concisely described in Laavan, the four stages of the union of the soul with God resulting in achievement of anand or bliss. The state of such a mind is described in the following shabad by Guru Teg Bahadur Ji on page 633:

"Jo nar dukh meh dukh naheen maanay.
Sukh sneh aur bhai naheen ja kai kanchan maattee maanay.
Nahee nindiaa nahee ustat jaakay lobh moh abhimaanaa.
Harkh soag tay rahay niaaro nahee maan abhimanaa.
Aassaa mansaa sagal tiaagay jag tay rahay nirasa.
Kam krodh teh parsay naahin titt ghat Brahm niwaasaa.
Gur kirpaa jeh nar kau keenee teh eh jugat pchaanee.
Nanak leen bhaio Gobnd sio jio paanee sang paanee." p-633

That man, who in the midst of grief does not feel pain, who is not affected by pleasure, affection or fear, and who looks alike upon gold and dust; who is not swayed by either slander or praise, nor affected by greed, attachment or pride; who remains unaffected by joy and sorrow, honor and dishonor; who renounces all hopes and desires and remains desire-less in the world; who is not touched by sexual desire or anger within his heart, God dwells in that man, blessed by Guru's Grace, understands the way. O Nanak, he merges with the Lord of the Universe, like water with water.

Now some general comments on spirituality:

1. Thinking and living in sat gun is virtuous living in Maya but not spirituality, which starts to come when one hears the anhad sabad and sees the vision of the soul/satguru inside (in sunn samadhi).
2. Spiritual knowledge comes when one meets the spirit/guru within: "Gian anjan Gur deea" p-293, but not just by reading spiritual books. Reading such books and discussing on this subject is sat gun which will help lead one to spirituality if one follows the advice of the Guru.
3. Gian in gurbani means spiritual knowledge and not intellectual knowledge acquired by reading or listening to intellectuals.
4. Sabad in Gurbani means anhad sabad which one hears when spiritually elevated on the spiritual path. This does not mean the written words of Gurbani.
5. Sabad guru in Gurbani means the anhad sabad which one hears in sunn samadhi. This is the sabad which leads us to the union with God, whereas, Gurbani Guru guides us and shows us the path to adopt to reach Sabad Guru. Gurus in the human body form came to guide and help by instructing us in our language, living the life they wanted us to live, and leaving behind the instructions in Gubani as our Eternal Guru in the written word.
6. We can be very wise and highly intellectualized with academic degrees but that does not help us on the spiritual path: "Sehas siaanpa lakh hoay taa ik naa chalay naal" p-1. Guru Ji clearly advises us to give up all our cleverness and in humility fall on the feet of the Guru to seek his blessings on this spiritual path; "Sabhay shad siaanpaa Gur kee pairee pa-ay" p-43.
7. Most of us are affected by reading Christian values of spirituality and other Western thoughts on spirituality which are based on Occidental philosophies in which spirituality is being in sat guna and does not take us beyond sat gun of Maya.
8. Scientific techniques have influenced us to believe only if one can observe and this idea is leading us to atheism or a secular humanism philosophy. However, Sikh teachings help us experience the Spirit and live spiritually by living in sat gun

and visualizing the spirit within us through Naam japna/simrna under the guidance of Gurbani and the help of holy company. The highest duty of a human is to do japna on the Name of God and perform pure deeds:

"Sarab dharam meh shresht dharam.
Har kaa Naam Jap nirmal karam." p-266

SPIRITUAL IGNORANCE

We are all spiritual beings, children of One Infinite God, living in this physical body which is time and space bound and, hence, finite. We, identifying ourselves with the body, create ignorance of this reality and misunderstanding that we are just physical and finite beings. This doubt and duality thus created between us and the Pure Self, the Divine Consciousness within, is called Spiritual Ignorance. In this ignorance, pain and doubt develops within, which is like a screen separating us from God:

"Andar agiaan dukh bharam hai vich parda door payeeaas." p-40

Unseen, God sits deep within the Self and cannot be realized as the veil of ego intervenes. In emotional attachment to Maya, the whole world is asleep. How can this doubt can be dispelled?

"Anatar Alakh naa jaee lakhiaa vich parda haumay paai.
Maya moh sabh soiaa eho bharam kahau kion jaee." p-205

The spiritualy ignorant person is called 'manmukh' in Gurbani and are blind to the reality of their real self:

"Jee kee saar na janee manmukh agianee andh." p-959

It is like an ocean's wave to think that it is separate from the ocean due to its ignorance. The wave cannot exist without the ocean. Superimposition of our bodily consciousness onto the Self gives rise to the world of names and forms. Pure Consciousness, God, is formless because it is beyond the limited body, mind and intellect. This separation between us and reality leads to spiritual ignorance. This is caused by Maya and we become attached to the material which causes duality:

"Eh Maya jit Har vsire moh upje bhaao duja laaia." p-921

In a mistaken identity one accepts the body as one's self and becomes bound to family, friends, material possessions, sense pleasures and so on. So the deluded man accepts the unreal to be real and the infinite to be finite. Due to the mental wilderness caused by such ignorance, one takes this world to be stable and permanent. Emotional attachment to Maya is totally painful and it is a bad bargain. Speaking falsly under the influence of Maya is like eating poison and it give rise to more evil in the mind:

"Maya moh sabh dukh hai khotta eh vapaaraa Ram.
Koor bol bikh khavnee bauh vadhe vikaaraa Ram." p-570

He who has spiritual ignorance within has intellect which is dull and dim, and he does not place his faith in the True Guru. He has deceit within himself and so he sees deception in all others. Through his deceptions, he is totally ruined. If blessed by God such a person will meditate on God's Name and be absorbed in the divine melody:

"Antar agiaan bhaee mut madham Satgur kee parteet nahee.
Andar kapat sabh kapto kar jaanay kapto khapeh khapee.
Satgur ka bhaanaa chitt naa aaveh aapnay sua-ay phiraaee.
Kirpaa karay je aapnee tun Nanak Sabad smaee." p-652

Spiritual wisdom is an antidote to ignorance. In other words, it is spiritual wisdom that can destroy the thick veil of ignorance. A breeze of spiritual wisdom cleans away the clouds of ignorance and we see the vision of reality:

"Nanak Gurmakh gian praapat haovay andher chukaaiaa." p-512

The darkness of ignorance is dispelled and spiritual wisdom lights the lamp of spiritual wisdom:

"Agiaan andheraa mitt gayaa gian deepaio." p-241

Gurbani promises us that if we make Naam japna our boat and install the intutive understanding of Gurbani as the boatman, God Himself will take us across this vast ocean of ignorance. Gurbani reminds us to make this boat now. The purpose of life is served for those who have acquired divine knowledge. This can be done by connecting our surti with Sabad through Naam Japna, love, devotion and good deeds. This will clean the accumulated dust of the past Karmas from the surface of the mind:

"Bhareeay mutt paapaan kay sung.
Oh dhopay Naavay ke rung." p-3

So join the Sat Sangat, sing God's glorious praises. With the sparkling jewel of spiritual wisdom, the heart will be illumined and the ignorance dispelled. The Sabad Guru within will give the healing ointment of spiritual wisdom which will dispel the darkness of spiritual ignorance. By Almighty's Grace one will meet a True Saint in whose company the mind will be enlightened:

"Gian anjan Gur deea agiaan andher binaas.
Har kirpa te Sant bhetiaa Nanak mun pargaas." p-293

Divine knowledge comes in by removing the ill effects of Maya from the mind with the help of Naam. The heart's lotus blossoms when Naam comes to abide by the heart:

"Gian mati kamal pargaas ttitt ghat Naamaiy Naam nivaas." p-1277

Once Naam/Sabad Guru/Satguru settles in the heart, one obtaines discriminating knowledge, which separates material knowledge from spiritual knowledge. The Guru reveals the spiritual knowledge of God:

"Bibek budh Satgur te paaee Gur giaan guru Prabh keraa." p-711

Once the ignorance is dispelled, the mind is purified of egoism and illumined with spiritual wisdom and its misunderstanding ends. When true wisdom arises, the unreality vanishes and only the One Pure, All Pervading Consciousness remains. In the remembrance of God are divine knowledge and the essence of wisdom:

"Prabh ke simran gian dhyaan tutt budh." p-262

SEEK GOD WITHIN

It is commonly believed that God is far away and generally thought to be living in Sach Khand. But is Sach Khand another zone or place in the universe where God lives? Although, the last Pauri in Jap Ji Sahib states that God lives in Sach Khand: "Sach Khand vassay Nirankar" p-8, it also tells us where Sach Khand is: "Tithe khand mandal varbhand je ko kathe ta ant na ant" p-8. All the planets, solar systems and galaxies are in Sach Khand and the extent of this creation is infinite. So God is everywhere in His universe and this is so on our planet earth, as well. But Gurbani states that He lives inside all, His created bodies: "Ghat ghat meh Harjoo bassay santan rahio pookar" p-1427. True Saints are telling this. So should we keep looking for Him outside? No. Gurbani tells us otherwise; why are you searching for God in the forest? Although, unattached yet He dwells everywhere and within you, too:

"Kahe re bun khojan jaee.
Sarabnivasee sadaa alaipaa tohee sang smaa-ee." p-684

The True One resides within us. Only the rare Gurmukhs, the God conscious persons, know about it:

"Ghar he andar Sacaha soee.
Gurmukh virla boojahay koee." p-1060

Ignorant persons seek Him in all directions but not within themselves. Attached to Maya they are bound by fear of death. The noose of death

94

around their neck will never be untied; in love of duality, they wander in reincarnation:

"Disantar bhavay antar nahee bhaalay Maya moh baadha jum kaalay. Jum kee phaasee kabhoo na tootay doojay bha-ay bharama-ayda." p-1060

All lies in the human body and nothing is outside. One who searches outside is deluded by doubts:

"Sabh kich ghar meh bahar nahee.
Bahar tolay so bharam bhulaee." p-102

I have found the True Lord searching within my body-village:

"Vich kaayaan nagar ladhaa Har bhaalee." p-1134

The mind lies within our body and the True One lies within the mind. Only those who become merged with the Truth seek and pursue Him within:

"Tun meh manooa mun meh Sacha.
So sacha mil Saachay racha." p-686

I am child of You O Father, God; and both of us reside in the same home, the human body:

"Haun poot Tera Too Baap mera.
Eko thaahar dohan baseraa." p-476

If God and mind, or the self, live in the same home within the body, why can't the mind meet with God and become one with Him? It is because there is a wall separating the two. Guru Ji calls it a wall of falsehood; 'koor thee pall'. It is a strong wall of false ego that separates the two even when they live together, like husband and wife:

"Dhan Pir ka ikhee sung vaasa vich haume bheet kraaree." p-1263

Mind thus polluted with this falsehood becomes impure and cannot merge with the True One who is Pure. Only through God's blessings it can meet with Him when He burns away this false ego with His Sabad:

"Mun maila Sach nirmalaa kio kar miliaa jaa-ay.
Prabh mailay taa mil ra-hay haumay sabad jlaa-ay." p-755

The Sabad, God's utterance, resounds in all beings. It is through this Sabad which connects the mind with God by destroying Maya which brings ego in the mind. This makes the mind a Gurmukh:

"Sub meh Sabad varte Prabh Saacha." p-1275
"Jeeaan andar jeeo Sabad hai jit Sauh milaava ho-ay." p-1250

So to connect with Sabad the mind has to go inside the body. For this, the consciousness has to be brought in so that it can hear Sabad which belongs to the Soul/Naam, which is a part of God within the body. When our mind is exposed to Naam, it then shines inside like millions of suns. By this, the mind is purified of all the dirt of Maya so that it becomes eligible to meet with God after His Grace falls on it.

The space inside where Naam lives is called the 'sookham moorat' or the subtle body in which Naam/Soul/Sabad live. This subtle body is enclosed inside the physical body:

"Sookham moorat Naam Niranjan kaayaan kaa akaar." p-466

Consciousness has to go in that space to hear Sabad, seek Naam and finally be blessed to meet God. To go into that space mind has to become totally thoughtless or go into sunn smaadh. It is in this place of sunn smadh that the True One lives. Satguru tells us so in Gurbani. The True one lives in this cave in sunn-smadh:

"Satguru tay paa-ay veechaaraa sunn smaadh Sachay ghar baaraa."
p-1037
"Sunn smaadh gufaa te aasan kewal Brahm pooran teh basan." p-894

Now how to reach that cave of sunn smaadh? That is where Naam japna/simran/dhiaunaa comes into the picture. The sole purpose of Naam Japna is to concentrate the mind on the sound of Gurmantra which is recited cyclically with devotion till the mind becomes so absorbed in it that it disconnects itself from the five senses and its consciousness (or surti) and goes inside. The mind is said to have gone into sunn and, the body into smaadhi, when it loses its awareness of its surroundings. The first such experience may last for a few minutes and should be repeated daily with Naam Japna, for which the best time recommended is Amrit Vela or early morning (three hours before sunrise) when the nature is quiet and very conducive to this spiritual exercise. After regular daily practice on it, one day the mind will hear the Sabad inside. The mind must focus its attention on it and this will start cleansing the mind of Mayan filth:

"Mun dhovo Sabad laago Har sio raho chit laa-ay." p-919

This stage of experience is refered to in Gurbani as bathing in Amritsar and it brings peace and health to both mind and body:

"Kar isnaan simar Prabh apnaa mun tun hoay arogaa." p-611

This also prepares the mind to see the vision of the Soul (Jot, a light), which is also the true identity of mind:

"Mun too Jot saroop hai apnaa mool paihchaan." p-411

This is followed by the brilliant vision of Naam which is like the light of millions of suns, which washes away all the doubts and spiritual darkness of the mind:

"Naam japat kot soor ujiaara binse bharam andheraa." p-700

Mind, at this stage, has to wait for Gurparsaad to unite with Parmaatmaa/Hari/Raam/ Gobind/ Sach/ Nirankaar/ Waheguru. After His Grace, one goes into Sehaj state and the doors of Nij Ghar/ Sehaj Ghar opens where nothing but bliss and peace is and our own true home exists.

This is what Guru Nanak Ji came to show us- the path to our real home, and he promised us total bliss and freedom full of love. There ends our miseries of going through the cycle of births and deaths. But we have to work for it by living in truthful thoughts, words and deeds. Guru Ji promises to connect us with his Guru, which is Sabad Guru, whom resides in us all and takes care of us beyond that level till we connect with Naam. Henceafter, we are connected with Ik Ounkar, having gone through Sunn Manadal, Sookh Mehal, Parkaash Mehal and finally land in Sach Mehal with our Divine Father:

"Satgur sikh ko Naam dhan deh.
Gur kaa Sikh vadbhaagee heh." p-286

This is what our Father offers us if we give ourselves to Him; the whole universe:

"Jay too meraa hoay rahen sub Jug teraa hoay." p-286

The choice is ours. What do we want? A little piece of land here on this planet earth for a short while or the whole universe forever and to sit with the Lord of the Universe on His Throne as His son:

"Ab to jaa-ay charay singhaasan milay hai sarang panee.
Ram Kabeera ek bha-ay hain koay naa chhakay pachanee." p-969

BE A GURSIKH
BECOME KHALSA
WAHEGURU'S OWN
JOIN HIM ON HIS THRONE
UNIVERSE IS KHALSA RAAJ

WAKE O MIND!

Gurbani repeatedly reminds us to awaken our mind. Is our mind asleep? We have to look into Gurbani further to get this answer from Guru Ji. When our body goes to sleep after a hard day's work, we lie down, close our eyes and soon we are totally oblivious to what is going on around us. In this state, we consider ourselves to be sleeping. We stop receiving any input from the five sensory organs of the body and are not aware of ourself. So sleeping is natural and is a temporarily loss of physical awareness of our body and its surroundings. When awake, we become aware of our body and what is happening around us. So being awake is gaining reality, or full awareness of our physical body, and its surroundings. So, when Guru Ji tells us that our mind should wake up, that means it must be sleeping and unaware of its reality. Wake up, O Mind. Why are you sleeping unaware of your true self?

"Jaag leho re manaa jaag leho kahe gafal soiaa." p-726

Wake up O now, sleeping mind. While you are sleeping unaware and wasting this life, the thieves (five doots of Maya) are stealing away your wealth (spiritual) from your house:

"Ab mun jagat rahau re bhaee.
Gafal hoaykay janam gwaaio chor moosaiy ghar jaee." p-739

Wake, O mind, you got to be awake. Without the Lord, nothing else is of any use to you; false are the emotional attachments and useless are the worldly entanglements:

"Jaag re mun jaganhaaray.
Bin Har avar na aavas kaamaa jhoothaa moh mithiaa psaaray." p-387

Mind is asleep, fascinated by Maya:

"Mun soiaa maya bismaad." p-182

In fact, we are our mind. Guru Ji addresses us also directly. In emotional attachment to- Maya the whole world is asleep. How could their doubts be dispelled?:

"Maya moh sabho jug soiaa.
Eh bharam kahau kion jaee." p-205

Man sleeps uselessly, intoxicated by Maya; he does not come to realize or understand reality:

"Bikaar Maya mud soiaa soojh boojh na aavay." p-408

Ignorant world is blind, O brothers; those who sleep are plundered:

"Agiaani jagat andh hai bhaaee sootay ga-ay muhaee." p-603

From above, it is obvious that the mind is intoxicated, fascinated and deluded by Maya which causes duality and bewilderment or the loss of memory of its true being. It forgets its true spiritual nature and is asleep to it, but is awake to material consciousness. It is from this spiritual slumber that Guru Ji is trying to wake it. The true nature of mind is 'Jot saroop' or personification of the Light of Soul inside the body: "Mun too Jot saroop hain apnaa mool pachaan." p-441. The duty of the mind is to find its true identity as the Divine Light under which it had 'Bibek Budhi', or spiritual discerning intelligence. Having lost it, it falls to material consciousness or becomes a 'manmukh', which brings the annihilation of spiritual life.

The subtle pull of Maya, the physical world, enchants the mind to it and makes it forget its true reality without the mind knowing about it. Only rare ones know about such a loss:

"Eh Maya jag mohiaa virla boojhay ko-ay." p-495

Maya, the enticer, has captivated the whole world with its three gunas. Everyone is engrossed in greed of the temporary, physical world:

"Mohini mohay leeay trai guna.
Lobh viaapee jhoothee dunia." p-1004

The teachings of Gurbani (Gurmat) stresses our continued efforts on the Inner/ Spiritual awakening of our mind by having virtuous thoughts, words and deeds, our constant remembrance on the Name of God, love and devotion to God and caring for and serving His creation as well as the acceptance of His Will. Guidance from Gurbani and the help of living True Saints, or Awakened Souls, is absolutely essential for the Spiritual Awakening of the mind. These Gurmukhs know this difficult terrain and have crossed Bhavjal Sagar, or the Ocean of Life of our incessant thoughts in our mind, which are so entangled in the material world.

The following Gurbani quotes will illustrate these points:

"Gurmukh aap pchaania Harinaam vassia mun aa-ay.
Andin bhagti ratiaa Harinaame sukh paa-ay." p-162

A Gurmukh is self-realized or has an awakened mind. God's Name comes to dwell within his mind. Imbued to God's Name night and day, he merges in peace and happiness. The devoted ones keep chanting 'Vaaho, Vaaho' while going to sleep and while becoming awake:

"Saunde vaho vaho uchrah uthday bhee vaho krain." p-319

Gurmukhs are blessed with Naam/Sabad which has the capability of destroying Maya in the mind:

"Maaya kaa maaran Sabad hai gurmukh paaya jaa-ay." p-8

Nanak says that it is the Sabad, the utterance of God within us, that destroys the veil of Maya on the mind. Only the Gurmukhs, the Awakened Beings, have gained access to this Sabad:

"Sadhsangat parsaadee santan kai soiou mun jaagio." p-215

By the grace of the True Saints (Awakened Beings), my sleeping mind has awakened:

"Mun tun budhi arpee Thakur ko tab hum sahaj soeay." p-214

When I dedicated my mind, body and intellect to God, I began to sleep in peace:

"Yayaa jaaro durmat do-oo.
Tisay tiaag sukh sehjay so-oo." p-253

Yayaa: Burn away duality and evil-mindedness. Give them up and sleep in peace and poise. Yayaa: Go seek the sanctuary of True Saints, the Awakened Ones. They will help you cross this world's ocean of Maya (awaken your mind):

"Yayaa ja-ay parro Sant sarnaa.
Jeh asar eh bhavjal tarnaa." p-253

Lord has blessed me with His Naam and purified my mind. Unstruck Divine Music is sounding in my inner self. I sing praises of the Glorious Lord with love and devotion. Lord has honored His humble servant. Destiny based on good deeds of my past life has come into effect. My mind has awakened from the slumber of countless past lives:

"Deeno Naam keeo pavit. Baajay anhad baajaa.
Rasik rasik Har gun gaaveh. Harjan apnay Gurdev nivaajaa.
A-ay banio purbalaa bhaag. Janam janam ka soiaa jaag." p-892

Manmukhs who are still under the hold of Maya are being plundered by its five doots (kaam, krodh, lobh, moh, hanker). Whereas Gurmukhs, the Awakened Ones, are safe and sound:

"Manmukh soay rahay se lootay Gurmukh saabat bhaee hay." p-1024

Self realization is the awakening of our mind from sleep, caused by delusion from attachment to Maya. The awakened mind finds its true nature as the spiritual child of God with Divine Radiance emanating from it. Its true spiritual discriminating intellect, the Bibek Budhi, returns and it can sort the Truth from the false (maya). It is in this awakened state that the mind becomes Gurmukh and acquires Gurmat. This spiritual stage is also called 'Chautha Pad'/ Turiya Awastha/Daswaan Dwaar/Begampura/Siv kee Puri/Sehaj Ghar, etc. in Gurbani. The entire Gurbani descended to us through such Awakened Minds who were ordained by God Himself.

To understand Gurbani in its truest sense, one has to awaken the mind to this level to comprehend the spiritual depiction presented therein. This is the reason Guru Ji asks the True Saints to disseminate this spiritual knowledge, 'akath katha', to people:

"Kahe Nanak suno Santo kathio akath khanee." p-918

SCIENCE AND RELIGION

The subject of Science and Religion is often brought up for discussion by scientific minded persons, who under its influence are turning atheist. They are afraid to admit that they are atheist but write about God to prove that atheists can also be spiritual. They question the existence of God stating that there is no scientific proof of it. They openly deny the existence of the soul and the mind as both are an extension of God within us. The soul is God Himself: "Atam Ram Ram hai Atam" in all of God's creation. The mind is a subtle manifestation of the Soul or Jot: "Mun too Jot saroop hain." These people's opposition to reincarnation and the after life is based on their lack of belief in the existence of the soul.

A scientific person's belief is Humanism which is atheism presented in a milder form which they often endorse as religion for the modern or scientific man. If we have to follow them, we will have to reject a majority of Gurbani's principles and declare ourselves to be atheists. They are against Khanday Thee Pauhal, Naam, Naam Japna and Sikh Rehat Maryada. For them, Guru Nanak was just a philosopher, so his Gurbani is just concepts which are liable to change with scientific advancement.

Their object is to dilute the faith of new generations of Sikhs to atheistic beliefs which they believe in so strongly. I often hear Sikhs complaining about RSS, Arya Smaj and other Babas polluting the Sikh principles. I think we are overlooking the danger from within our own Sikh society. The scientific man's attacks start with creating doubts about all the historical writings of Sikhs at the time of the Gurus, like Bhai Gurdas and later writers of the eighteenth and nineteenth centuries. Anything spiritual that they do not understand is called it a METAPHOR or VEDANTIC as if the Vedas were written by heretics. The Guru Ji often refers to the Vedas and declares these to be dictated by God to Brahma:

"Chaaray Baid Brahma kau deeay parh parh karay beecahr." p-424
Science deals with the knowledge of physical nature whereas religion deals with spirituality. Religion shows us how to practice spirituality while living in the physical world and teaches us how to realize our self and God, the source of spirituality. Science has no beliefs or tools to measure spirituality, which is Naam and the spiritual forces which run the universe under the Hukam or Will of God. The Laws of Nature discovered by scientists are related to the physical world and its forces can be measured by tools. The scientists have no tools to measure spiritual forces as they belong to the spiritual domain of God's creation. Naam Japna as advised by Gurbani can take you into the spirit zone called sunn where Naam, Sabad, Soul and God, our True Home Nij Ghar and Sach Ghar, the Home of the True One is:

"Satgur tay paa-ay veechaaraa.
Sunn smaadh Sachay Ghar baaraa." p-1037

For an atheist, the brain is the mind but the brain happens to be a physical organ in the body. The brain takes input from the sensory organs to the mind and then transmits the output of the mind to the action organs of the body. The body is then able to conduct the physical deeds as planned by the mind for results of which the mind has planned to do. All the thinking of the mind reflects in brain activity which can be measured by electronic signals. So, it is assumed that the brain is the mind. In the case of near death experiences when body is declared to be clinically dead, the brain shows no activity. But when the body becomes alive again, the person tells about all of what was going on during the period when body was considered dead. The observer or consciousness was outside the body and observed all the events. The mind remembered everything when the body was not conscious or, otherwise, clinically dead.

All of the spiritual phenomena are outside the observation range of the tools of the scientists. But that does not mean it is not there. Scientists simply cannot record and experience it. For them it does not exist. But for a spiritual person, all this is as visible and understood as any physical phenomena to the ordinary person. Ask the Gurus and Bhagats in Gurbani who are telling their direct experience of visions of God and describing the spiritual world:

"Jeh jeh pekhon teh hajoor door katohn na jaaeen." p-677

The so called modern, scientific people or atheists are denying all of this because they cannot gauge or measure God, which they consider is only energy (which is measurable). But can they measure God's energy?

The whole universe, physical and spiritual, visible or invisible, is the creation of God who is running it under His Hukam or Will: "Hukmay andar sabhko bahar Hukam na koay." Nature is both His physical and spiritual world. Many laws relating to the physical world have been recognized by scientists and they call these the Laws of Nature.

These laws relate to forces: mechanical, gravitational, frictional, hydraulic, electrical, magnetic, electromagnetic, etc. Development of science, the industrial revolution, and new technologies are based on these forces and laws. However, all these laws relate to the physical world only. These laws are not effective on spiritual forces, which are independent of these and are under the direct Will of God at the consciousness plane.

There are laws for the spiritual world which are executed by God through His separate organization under the Judge Dharam Raj and his team of Chittar Gupt, the observer, and Jumdoot, the spiritual police assigned to each live being, as described in Gurbani. Only Gurmukhs who have become one with God can see them. For the common person these spiritual laws won't be true and for an atheist who does not believe in God and the soul, they do not exist and are only metaphors; but metaphors for what? Guru Ji calls the spiritual world and this world as: 'halat, palat', 'eet, oot', 'aagay, pacchay'. It is in the sunn zone, the etheric space where lies Nij Ghar, Sach Ghar, Sookh Mehal, Dev Lok. It is in this world that other spirits, like angels, and those spirits, waiting for their next reincarnation, exist. They are all under God's Hukam or Will. Hukam mentioned in Gurbani also relates to us; our mind and soul and their journey in this world and the other world.

Religion in no way contradicts science, but it is scientists who are turning away from spirituality and becoming atheist or humanist or agnostic. Scientists openly advertise and debate that there is no God. As a scientist and engineer myself, I do admire the great achievements of the dedicated work of many a scientist around the world who have contributed to the welfare of humanity at large. Notwithstanding, the side effects of some of their products are very serious and we have to be worried about these. But the biggest side effects of all their work has been the evaporation of people's faith in God and spirituality. As they have started to think that they are independent of any control or Hukam of God, these people have let moral discipline fall into the hands of the five doots of Maya. In this respect, scientists have let go of the advantage of the most powerful forces available to human who are struggling hard against the gross material forces. When spiritual people use those forces people call these actions miracles, but scientists do not believe them. It is like the prodigal son who ran away from home and came back having lost it all. The father still accepted him back. Have we forgotten that this intelligence which we think is ours is all given by God: 'Sikh matt sabh budh tumaaree' and that we are only as smart as the intelligence He gives:

"Jaisee too matt deh taisee ko paavay." p-351

God is speaking through Gurbani to readers: 'All the creatures are mine (God's) and I live within all of them. Who can make one understand something when I have confused him? Who can confuse the man whom I have shown the way? Whom I have misguided on the path, nobody can show him the path':

"Sabh ghat mairay haun sabhnaa andar jisay khuaee tis kaun khay.
Jisay dikhaavaan vaatree tisay bhulaavay kaun.
Jisay bhulaee pandh sir tisay dikhaavay kaun." p-952

I do not see any conflict between science and religion as they belong to two different zones of the creation of God. Some scientists, however, do not accept the spiritual zone and, hence, deny the need of faith in God, the soul, the mind and life in the spiritual world. They are welcome to have their beliefs but should not confuse the gullible or hurt other people's faith by misinterpreting Gurbani to prove their belief system to be correct and propagate Humanism as Gurmat.

LOGIC IN RELIGION AND SPIRITUALITY

Logic is very important for the implementation of spiritual principles in our day-to-day life in order to make sure that our application is not composed simply of baseless rituals. Whichever way we profess our religion, there should be a sound reason for the practice. In fact, that is what Guru Ji did. All the baseless rituals were taken out after defining the spiritual foundations for Sikhism and were then taught to the followers of Sikhi so they could then live their lives according to these principles. The religious service was then reduced to sitting in sangat and doing kirtan, Naam Japna, giving a discourse on spiritual principles and sharing a meal together afterward. The priestly class was discarded in Sikhi as every human being was considered a child of God and could pray directly to Him who resides within everybody also:

"Ghat ghat meh Harjoo basay." p-86

Unfortunately, we have recreated the position of the priest in our Gurdwaras and have started depending upon them for our prayer. We now rely on them to do 'paath' for us, such as 'akhand paath' or 'sehaj paath', as if they are the ones closer to God. In fact, we have given up complete control of our Gurdwaras to them and they are the ones managing it instead of the elected committees. We have also started observing sangraand, massiaa, chaleesaa (going to gurdwara for forty days for a special wish, hoping it will be granted by doing this), serving special dinner to the 'granthees' (similar to 'sraadh' given to Brahmins), 'kathakaars' to tell us tales instead of briefing us on Gurmat, offering money and other physical things to 'granthee's' as if this act will please God. Our granthees have become just like 'brahmins' who were discarded by Guru Nanak. Instead of us doing kirtan, we have given it up to ragee jathas, most of them do not even know any raag and we still call them ragees and think they are holy people because they sing gurbani. The whole system has totally degenerated into what was there before Guru Nanak. Whatever katha Granthis do, we accept it because we do not know much about it. The Sikhi we learn from them is the Sikhi they have picked up from few books they have read, the dera or a manmukh school they studied at prior. The whole practice in the Gurdwara is somehow designed to create income for the Granthees, Pathees, Keertanias and the committee.

But no logic is needed for our spiritual development and progressing to the ultimate goal of us realizing God. Do not be surprised -please read on. On the path to realizing God, our intellect and knowledge gained of the physical world is of no help as now we are dealing with the spiritual arena where only instructions from Gurbani will lead us. They are: "Tun mun dhun sabh saup Gur ko hukam maneeay paaeeay" p-918, "Mun baichay Satgur ke paas tis sewak ke karaj raas." p-1258. Here "dhun" is the number of breaths or time God gives us on this planet. It is in this game of love where we have to give up everything we have in order to seek the truest of love. We have to give up all our cleverness and worldly knowledge in order to accept the instructions of the Guru without question:

"Sabhe shad siaanpaa Gur ki Pairee paaiay." p-431
Follow the path Guru has shown you and do whatever he tells you to do:

"Gursikh meet chalo Gur chalee.
Jo Gur kahe soee bhal maanio." p-667

It is not easy to leave all possessions and the ego behind, but there is no other way to that realm about which we know nothing. To get the Gurmat we have to give up our 'munmatt' to enter that realm by remembering Har (the God) by doing Naam japna and keeping Him in our mind at all times:

"Mun ki mutt tiaago harjan eha baat kathaini.
Andin Har Har Naam dhiaavo Gur Satgur ki mutt laini." p-209

When we enter the stage of dhyan or sunn by doing Naam japna, our mind becomes thoughtless and has no consciousness of our body. Our knowledge is abandoned and we are completely (our body, mind and breath) in the hands of Sabad/Naam Guru. And this is who will guide us from that place of quietude so long as we are in sunn. The moment a thought comes up in our mind, we come out of sunn and are back in the world of Kaal/Maya and our regular intellect takes over -but our mind has been cleansed a little by the power of Naam: "Oh dhope Naave ke rang". Regular cleansing of our mind this way get us closer to our Source, the God, till one day our mind has become pure and is then ready for His grace- Gurparsad. When that happens we have made it to our natural home, Nij Ghar and have Naam in our mind instead of 'koor di pall'. The mind thus gets enlightened with countless suns, all doubts and spiritual darkness vanishes:

"Naam japat kot soor ujiaara binse bharam andheraa." p-700

It is the state of Anand which gives you the bliss after seeing the light of countless suns, and this is God Himself as Naam. This is what makes one a Jivanmukt and leads to the next step of Sehaj Ghar by God's Grace and we become one with our Father. This is the state of a Gurmukh.

Sant, Sadh, Bhagat and Brahmgiani are perfect beings helping us in spiritual progress on the way to Nij Ghar. Guru Ji repeatedly asks a Sikh to find the company of such a person who will guide the novice along the path of spiritual progress where intelligence does not work.

Such true saints may not be wearing garb of professional Sants, they work for their living and are not dependent on society. They help connect the seeker with Sabad Guru inside who imparts the spiritual knowledge which leads to Naam: "Gian Anjan Gur deea." One needs no logic on this path of Love and should be willing to die for Love.

Be a humble servant to all and be ready to die (by killing your false ego), giving up all hopes of material life, then tread on this path to your Love:

"Pehlaan maran kabool jivan ki shad aas.
Hoay sabna ki renuka tau aaao haamaaray paas." p-1102

It is an unknown and difficult path: "Chaal niraalee bhagtaan keri bikham maarag chalnaa", where our intellect and worldly wisdom does not work. Many-a-times, we try to interpret Gurbani using our intellect, logic and worldly-scientific knowledge. It only leads to gross misinterpretations and out of spiritual ignorance we fail to understand why we are wrong. The spiritually ignorant know not the path of love and, instead, they wander around being lost:

"Panthaa prem naa jaanaee bhoolee phiray gwaar." p-1426

SIKHS AND THEIR RELIGION

SIKHISM

A Sikh is a disciple or follower of a Divine Master who is spiritually enlightened. He is called a Guru in this new religion known as Sikhism. It is the youngest and the fifth largest major religion of the world with a global population of thirty millions. It is a monotheistic religion which started in Punjab, the northwest part of India. Guru Nanak introduced his followers to Sikhi as a messenger of God in 1469 AD near Lahore, which is now in Pakistan. Guru Nanak declared all human beings to be the children of One God and to be born equal. He forbade worship of idols as only God was to be worshipped through singing his praises and remembrance of His Name on a personal and congregational level. Guru Nanak's principles taught that God is the Creator of the entire universe and all life on it. God also resides in each of His creations and supports each and every one of them. Everything in the universe is running as per His will and plan- nothing is out of His control or surveillance. He gives consciousness, intelligence and guidance to each live being about their role in life. All physical life forms die at the specified time and reincarnate into either the same or become other forms as they are judged by the Creator.

The ultimate form created by Him on this planet is the human body. The only purpose of human life is to seek union of its soul with God and to achieve bliss and liberation from the cycle of births and deaths. This is only possible by being truthful in thought, word and deed, showing love and respect for God and all His creations. By adhering to these principles, we then connect with Him through daily practice of deep meditation in His Name and then wait for His Grace.

THE SIKH SCRIPTURE

There were nine more Gurus that followed Guru Nanak. Teachings, or utterances, of Gurus and thirty five other saints that had belonged to other faiths were compiled in Sikh Scripture called Granth Sahib. Guru Gobind Singh, the tenth Guru of the Sikhs, ended the line of Guruship in human body and declared Granth Sahib as Guru of the Sikhs for eternity in 1708 AD just before he departed for his heavenly abode. The Divine Message in Guru Granth Sahib is called Gurbani, and is written as hymns in sublime poetical form. It is separated into thirty one musical orders called Ragas in 1,430 pages, and is written in the new Gurmukhi script in the language of the gurus and saints.

KHALSA

Guru Gobind Singh, in 1699AD created a special initiation ceremony for the Sikhs to pledge their allegiance to this newly created religion. This ceremony is called Khande Thee Pauhal, in which water containing sugar is stirred with a double edged sword while reciting five prayers from the utterances of Sikh Gurus. When ready, it is offered to the devotees to drink from. The devotees drink it five times and the holy water is then sprinkled into their eyes and hair five times while they recite the Name of God, Waheguru, each time. They are told of the discipline to be followed in their daily life and their responsibility as a member of their newly adopted faith and Brotherhood of the Khalsa. Khalsa means: a pure one and belonging to God.

They are required to keep uncut hair, wear a steel bangle on the wrist of the right hand, a turban on their head, to wear a small sword symbolizing their responsibility as a soldier in the event of self defense and the defense of others. They are also required to wear long breeches and keep a wooden comb in their hair to keep them clean. Males are given then given the name Singh- which means a lion, and the ladies are given the name as Kaur- which means a princess.

Every initiated Sikh is required to meditate on the Name of the God early morning and say the prayers morning, evening and at bed time. They are required to lead a truthful life, earn their livelihood by honest means and share their earnings with others in order to help, serve and protect them. They are to join other Sikhs in the congregational prayers and participate in the community organized programs for service to others. Adultery and premarital sex is not permitted. They are also not to eat 'halal' meat prepared in the Moslem way. Smoking of tobacco and taking intoxicants, as well as other mind altering drugs, are strictly prohibited. If an initiated Sikh commits an offence by breaking any religious vow, there is a provision for confession where minor offences can be forgiven for a suitable penance. For a major offence, one has to go through the initiation ceremony again along with a suitable penance.

EQUAL STATUS FOR WOMEN

Women are given equal and respectful status in the family and community. She carries the prime responsibility of raising the children and passing on the Sikh values to them so that they grow up loved, cared for with positive attitude as responsible citizens and contribute to the welfare of the community and society at large. They are free to participate in social, cultural, religious and political arenas where they have made noteworthy contributions. They have proven their talents in the fields of fine arts, literature, education, science, sports and athletics.

GURDWARA : SIKH PLACE OF WORSHIP

The Sikh place of congregational worship is called Gurdwara: the doorway to the Guru. Visitors enter the prayer hall after taking their shoes off and covering their head with a scarf or wearing a turban.

They sit on the carpeted floor after paying their obeisance to the Guru Granth Sahib, which is laid open on a pedestal, covered with fine scarves under a canopy with an attendant sitting behind. The Divine Message of God is written in the hymns and is explained by the preacher and is then followed by hymn singers, forming the major part of the congregational service. There is no priestly class or clergy in Sikh religion. Any person that is well versed with the spiritual knowledge of the Scriptures can volunteer or can be hired to give a sermon. At the end of service, a prayer is said with congregation standing alongside with folded hands, asking for God's blessings of peace, love and harmony for those present in the congregation as well as for the entirety of humanity. 'Krah Parsad', a communion of sweet pudding, is served to all followed by Langar which is a free vegetarian meal in the community kitchen. The service is open to all visitors irrespective of their race or religion, regardless of whether they are members or not. Temporary lodging and boarding, if available, is provided free of charge to the guests in the building. The central Sikh shrine, known as the Golden Temple, is in the city of Amritsar in East Punjab, India.

SIKHS AS LIBERATORS

Sikhs played a major role in the freedom of India. This was first done in defending India from Middle Eastern rulers in the eighteenth century when the Sikhs successfully established their own secular kingdom in the north western part of the country in 1799 AD. They went on to rule for fifty years. Sikhs then defended India from British rulers in the twentieth century. Freedom was finally won in 1947 AD and India became a democratic Republic. Although, Sikhs are a small minority in India- bearing only two percent of the nation's population; they maintained forty seven percent of the armed forces in India during British rule. Sikhs then went on to help Britain fight in the First and the Second World Wars.

SIKHS IN DIASPORA

Sikhs are hard working and adventurous people and have moved to all parts of the world for better economic opportunities. With an independent spirit, dauntless courage, strength of their faith in God and hard work, Sikhs have become very much at home in the new lands they have migrated to. They have made significant contributions in the fields of engineering, medicine, science, computer technology, farming, skilled labor and the transportation industry. There are thirty million Sikhs worldwide, out of which twenty-three million are residing in India. The largest concentration of Sikhs outside India is in England, Canada, United States, East Africa and Malaysia. Their population is now growing in Australia, Europe and New Zeeland. In the United States, there are about half a million, in Canada there are about one and a quarter million, and in England about a million. In the United States, the only Indian congressman has been a Sikh, Dalip Singh Saund, in which he served during President Kennedy's time. In Canada, in spite of their small number, Sikhs are well represented at the State and Federal level as members of Parliament and State Senate. In England, too, there are Sikh members of the House of Commons and many have been honored by the Queen. The previous Prime Minister of India was Sikh, as was one of the Presidents, and one Commander in Chief of the armed forces for a few short years.

MISTAKEN IDENTITY PROBLEM

Recently, after the incidence of 9/11, they have been mistaken for people from the Middle East for the turban they wear and beard they keep. Due to this, they have been the victims of bias and hate crimes. Although, the Sikh community is trying to create awareness about their faith through interfaith meetings and media at a local level- the problem needs help at state and federal level to avoid unnecessary killings and violence against innocent Sikhs. To protect and serve others is the duty of law enforcement agencies, but that also happens to be the moral duty of a Sikh and they are willing to assist these agencies in this matter. Their homes, hearths and Gurdwaras are open to any person who seek help, shelter or are looking for a friendly hand.

PURPOSE OF HUMAN LIFE

When we are gifted with a child- a physical, human body at home; we feel very happy and thankful to God without caring what this human should do in life to make the best use of it. Parents do not get any instructions for the child. They probably do not care for these instructions. They just watch other people and follow them as if they know all about raising a child. The only thing they do plan for their son or daughter is that they should be raised physically all right and educated well enough to get a good job when they begin to work. That is, basically, the only criterion in a parent's mind and the world accepts it. They do not know that their spiritual master, Guru Nanak, left them a message in the Guru Granth Sahib of what to do with this God given new life. This new life which came to them on this land is called by the Guru as Dharam Khand; the new arrival's actions, words and thoughts will be judged for their entire life. Good deeds, thoughts, words and remembering God only wins His favor of meeting Him and rids this new earthly life of punishment in the form of cycles of deaths and births. This goes on until we win His favor and enter God's true house after death for peace and bliss. So, the judge is the Creator God and not the people. He advises the parents and the new born child through Gurbani of Guru Nanak. God even took care of you in the womb of your mother, keeping you alive by making you do simran in His Name: "Maat garabh mehn Apna simran deh tai tum rakhnhare" p-613. In fact, He is the Father and the Mother of the child. He takes care of the baby who is His child:

"Har Ji Mata Har Ji Pita.

Harr Ji meri saar kare hum Har ke balak." p-1101

According to our destiny some are far and some are close to the blissful House of God. So the Guru Granth Sahib advises that in this life you have been born as a human (there are 8.4million kinds of species and the human body is at top of the list and one in which one can become one with God) so you have received a chance to meet the True One in this life. Other deeds you do (besides daily honest earnings for you, your family and home) are of no use to you except meditating on God's Name in the company of Holy:

"Bhaee praapat manukh dehuria. Gobind milan ki ehi teri bareea. Avar kaaj tere kitay naa kaam. Mil saadh sangat bhaj kewal Naam." p-12

You achieved this invaluable human life after wandering through 8.4 million lives. Nanak is advising you to earn and save Naam in this life, as you have entered this stage have come close to winning this goal:

"Lakh chaurasee bharmatian dulabh janam ab paaio ray.
Nanak Naam smahl toon so din nera aaio ray." p-1017

Man looks for security and happiness in earning big money. He thinks happiness lies in watching plays and stage shows. There is no happiness in earning more wealth in foreign lands, but all happiness lies in singing the praises of God:

"Sukh naheen bauhtay dhun khaatay. Sukh naheen paikhay nrit naatay.
Sukh naheen bauh des kamay. Sarab sukhaan Har Har gun gaa-ay." p-1047

Live a life of positive efforts and enjoy it with your honestly earned money. Meditating on the Name of God will win a union with Him. Nanak says all your worries will then leave you:

"Uddam krendiaan jeo toon kmaavdiaan such bhunch.
Dhiaandiaan toon Prabhu mil Nanak utri chint." p-1522

After a very long time, one has obtained this difficult to obtain human body. This body is going waste without Naam (spiritual wealth). Thus, without Naam this body is worse than a beast, demon or fool. This person does not even understand Him who created this body:

"Chrinkaal paaee durlabh deh. Naam vihooni hoee kheh.
Passoo pret mughad te buri. Tise naa boojhe jin eh siree." p-890

Guru Ji is warning us again and again that this body is made by God for man to reach Him through his mind. This mind has been given special spiritual powers to attain salvation, mukti, or become a jiwanmukat through Naam. Human birth is obtained because of lot of good deeds done in the past life. But without Naam life is cursed and wasted:

"Manas janam punn punn kar paaiaa.
Bin Naaven dhrig dhrig birthaa jaee." p-450

Man has wandered through 8.4 million incarnations before getting born as a human. In all these incarnations, he was once a rock or mountains; in so many incarnation he was aborted in the womb, and in so many incarnations he lived like a tree. In so many births he was a worm and an insect; in so many incarnations he was a bird and snake and, in so many incarnations, he was yoked like an ox and a horse. Time has come now to meet the Lord of the Universe. After a very long time, this human body was fashioned for you:

"Kaee janam bhaey keet patangaa. Kaee janam gaj meen kuranga.
Kaee janam pankhee sarap hoio. Kaee janam haiver brikh joio.
Mil Jagdish milan kee bareeaa. Chrinkaal eh deh sanjareeaa." p-126

Thus we have been everything God has created on this planet. We keep entering and departing through birth and death and keep repeating this cycle for our desires, again and again, without learning lessons from it. We go through happiness and grief for nothing and do not work to become liberated through Naam. This liberation results in no grief but a blissful life forever. But we never remember that life in the human body is given to us only to meditate on the name of The Lord, without fail, as this happens to be the only purpose.

I have seen the whole world but there is no peace or happiness without meditation on God. The body and money comes to an end searching for happiness but can't find it:

"Ditha sabh sansaar sukh na Naam bin.
Tun dhan hochee shaar jaane koee jan." p-201

In the end, I would like to emphasize again that there is no peace and happiness in this world without meditation on God. This is the only purpose of human life:

"Bhajo Gobind bhool mutt jaao.
Manas janam ka ehi laaho." p-1156

DHUR KI BAANI

Dhur Ki Baani is the utterance of God in Anhad Sabad. This is perceived by the Gurmukh, a person who is one with God, in Chautha Pad or Turia Avastha and expressed in their own language- spoken or written. The source of Dhur Ki Bani is God, Himself, who communicates to His children through Gurmukhs whether they are Sant, Sadh, Bhagat, Brahmgiani or Gurus:

"Sabday upjay amrit baani Gurmukh aakh sunaavania." p-125

Bhatts were also Gurmukhs and they sang in praise of Gurus like other Gurus sang in praise of their Guru and God; their ultimate Guru. Even God praises a Gurmukh who makes it to Sach Ghar after conquering the five doots of maya. He praises and hugs them:

"Dhan dhan shaabaash kahay harjan ko Nanak mail la-ay gal laee." p-493

Gurmukh, the one who speaks for the Guru or God, is above the three gunas of Maya and his utterance is called Naad- the sound of Anhad. God's Sabad and his sayings about spirituality and preaching is called Baani. Guru Nanak refers to this preaching as Vedun in the Sixth Pauri of the Japji Sahib. Ved meant Dhur ki Baani at the time. A Gurmukh is always absorbed in divine thoughts:

"Gumukh Nadun Gurmukh Veduun.

Gurmukh rahia smaaee." p-2

Bhaaee Gurdaas also calls Gurmukh's utterances as Naad and Baid; and that Gurmukh knows the Divine secrets:

"Gurmukh Naad Baid Gurmukh paavay bhed." Vaar-42

The Guru Granth Sahib is not a structured thesis written on Spirituality. Each hymn or shabad is complete lesson in itself. Each Raag is not a chapter with one subject to discuss but, Gurus and Bhagats give a complete lesson as to how to reach our Dhur through purification of our mind. This purification of the mind is obtained through truthful thoughts, words, deeds and the cleansing of it by connecting to Naam.

Sri Guru Granth is written as an ocean of spiritual knowledge for the seeker. It is not written as a book of science. Only ones who have full faith in Guru Ji and consider Gurbani as Dhur Ki Baani can make the best use of it. Looking for faults in the divine utterance simply lowers the status of Satguru to that of an ordinary human being. Guru Ji advises us to treat the Baani of Satguru as Truths spoken through the mouths of Gurmukhs by God Himself:

"Satgur ki Bani Sat Sat kar jano Gursikho.
Har karta aap muhon kdhaa-ay." p-308

Persons without the Guru even stay away from those persons who talk ill of the Guru:

"Jo Gur gopay aapnaa tis dithay niguray sharmaa-ay." p-308

So, we are advised by Guru himself. If we call someone our Guru or Satguru, they deserve the utmost respect from our heart and we should cherish their divine utterances as statements of truth on spirituality.

If Guru Ji gave Bhagats and Bhatts a place to sit with themselves as equal, what right do Sikhs have to question the Divine Guru's decision when we as humans stand nowhere near them? Let us seek their blessings by submitting to them in humility and the utmost reverence.

IK OUNKAAR

Sri Guru Granth Sahib starts with IK OUNKAR. From the times of the Gurus till now it has been pronounced exactly the same way. But now, we have some scientific Sikhs and self acclaimed scholars who have invented a new pronunciation for it as IK-OH or IK-BEANT. Because 'oora' is open and it should be pronounced as OH and, since it is extended, it could also be pronounced as BEANT. Through using phonetics, this is scientific, logical and rational pronunciation of the first letter of Gurbani in the SGGS; a scripture on Sikh spirituality perceived by Guru Nanak- a messenger of God and other Sikh Gurus.

Some may doubt the oral tradition but, if the Guru writes it as Ounkar, should we doubt it and dare to pronounce it as IK OH or IK OH BEANT? I wonder what these scientists are trying to prove other than the Guru being wrong in writing it as OUNKAR.

There is a definite meaning to have an open and extended 'oora'. The first sound God ever uttered in the Anhad Sabad is 'Ooo------un', written as open 'oora'and then extended and pronounced as kaar- which is the infinite physical creation by God.

So IK OUNKAAR means: The ONE who through His SABAD (o--un) is manifested throughout His infinite creation (kaar).

This is furtherer explained in Gurbani. God created His universe by uttering just one word:

"Keeta passao eko kwaao." p-3

This Sabad is also called Naam in Gurbani. God first created Naam from which He created His Nature, or physical universe, and is sitting in each one of His creations as Sabad or Naam and relishes it:

"Aapinay aap saajio aapinay rachio Naaon.
Dooey kudrat saajiay kar assan ditho chaao." p-463

Guru Ji has written Ounkar at tens of places within the SGGS and he wrote it for God. He (keertania) sings of One Infinite Creator Lord, and the tune of the One Lord:

"Ounkar ek dhun ekay raag allaapay." p-885

The Infinite Lord creates the universe. He created days and nights:

"Ounkar utpaatee.
Keea dinas aur ratee." p-1003

The Anhad Sabad of God created the entire universe:

"Oooun sabh shrisht upaaee." p-1061

The Infinite Creator Lord is manifested in His creation and He will merge into that:

"Onkar eko dhun rahiaa Eko meh smaavego." p-310

What is the difference if Ounkaar is written in Hindu scriptures as OM and Guru Nanak Dev Ji calls it Oounkaar in the Guru Granth Sahib? This is the sound of the first utterance of God. What makes it Hindu or Sikh? Guru ji constantly uses Hindu names of Gods. So is he preaching Hindu Gods to us? Same thing goes for Brahma, Vishnoo and Mahesh whom the Hindus worship as gods. Guru Ji acknowledges their creation by God in Jap Ji Sahib in the 30th Pauri:

"Eka maaee jugat viaee tin cheley parvaan.
Ik sansaari ik bhandaari, ik laa-ay dibnaan." p-2

These three chelas, or sons, of Maya were given the assignment of creation, preservation and death and were later on given the names as Brahma, Vishnoo and Mahesh. Was God creating Hindu gods? These three gods work for God and some people have started worshipping them. Guru Ji warns us very clearly that we must be blind and ignorant to forget the Husband Lord and worship servants, instead:

"Thakur chhod daasi ko sevay manmukh andh agianaa." p-1138

Problems in name usage also exists for Hari Mandir, which means God's Abode. Do Hindus have monopoly over the name Hari and Mandir? Guru Ji himself uses Hari Mandir in reference the human body as God lives in it:

"Hari Mandir eh sareer hai." p-1346

It is this Vedantic phobia in the minds of few that is creating this confusion amongst the Sikhs resulting in many trying to disown what Guru Ji is preaching as truth- even if their name happens to be in Vedas or other shaashtraas. Guru Ji did not come to null and void the truths given in earlier scriptures but he did correct some wrong beliefs and practices such as meaningless rituals. The Guru gave the people a very practical religion and has shown the correct way to reach our Source, or Dhur, through Naam as well as how to defend ourselves and others with the Kirpan.

What are we so afraid of? If Gursikhi lived through five difficult centuries- what can happen now when the whole world is watching now with what goes on any where else? Have we lost faith in Guru Ji? Do we think Sikhi belongs to us, the poor weaklings? SIKHI BELONGS TO GURU NANAK AND GURU GOBIND SINGH, who created it under the orders of WAHEGURU.

So please have faith and stop making blasphemous statements to prove your scholarship or by becoming a Galilee of the Age of Science. Gurus and Gurbani is perfect and stop looking to find faults in it. If you are a Sikh of the Guru, have faith in the Guru and seek his blessings for Gurmat.

BE BRAVE

BE A LION

IS GOD ENERGY

It is very convenient for scientific minded persons to define God as energy. God, being the Creator that He is, and energy is required to make things in the physical world- so God must be the energy. And then they connect God to energy equations like Einstein's E=MC2 and other energy laws of conversion of energy developed by scientists during the last two centuries. It sounds so logical to them. We know and understand the energy forms relationship with matter- but do we know God and what kind of energy He is and whether that is convertible to the energies known to us? If we do not know God, should we not approach the ones who met and experienced God and see what they say about Him? But I see we get carried away by our little bit of knowledge of the physical matter gained so far and we begin to start defining God using it. Is He a physical energy which is convertible to the one we have come to know? Knower of Truth, Gurus and Bhagats from Gurbani do not say so.

According to Gurbani God is a spirit, Paramatama, who is the Creator of the universe and energy in it. He first created Naam/His Utterance/ Anhad Sabad and through it created rest of the universe and pervades in it and enjoys His creation:

"Aapeenay aap saajio aapeenay rachio Naon. Dooee kudrat sajeeay kar aasan ditho chao." p-463

"Naamay he tay sabh kich hooaa." p-753

"Ek kwaa-ay te sabh hoaa." p-1003

It was Naam which created the rest of the physical universe which brings forth live beings and puts them to work as God wanted:

"Jee jant sabh Tudh upaa-ay.
Jit jit bhaanaa tit tit laa-ay." p-103

Naam created five basic components of creation (air, water, fire -energy, solid matter-earth and sky-ether):

"Panch tatt kar tudh shrisht sabh sajee." p-736

So God is the Creator of energy through Naam. So energy is His creation. Can energy be God? Does energy have the divine qualities of God such as consciousness, intelligent, wisdom, compassion, love, grace etc? No, it does not have those qualities. Only Naam has it and it sits within each live being as Soul. Energy is only a component used by God for creation of the physical world. Can it be the Creator? I wonder why we keep calling it as God. We state so by total disregard of Gurmat or Gurbani. Although, we do not call ourselves atheist but we do act like them often and yet we think we are spiritual. I have read in some places that atheism is a religion (of non believers) but never heard that atheists (not believing in the spirit) could be spiritual.

Some of us will stick to our statement that God is energy or shakti. So we become sakats-worshipper of shakti. Let us see what Gurbani says about sakat-the energy worshippers or faithless cynics.

Sakat, the faithless cynic, has never tasted the divine elixir. Ridden by ego and is always bitten by it from within. He suffers with it when alive and when dead is beaten on his head by the angel of death:

"Sakat Har rus saad na jaania tin antar haumay kandaa hay.
Jio jio chalay chubhay dukh paavay jumkaal sahay sir dandaa hay."
p-13

The sakat does not like the truth; false are the foundations of the false:

"Saakat sach na bhaavaee korai koori paa-ay." p-22

O Lord, let me not be in the company of the saakat who is already cursed by You, The Creator:

"Har saakat sang naa karioh oay maaray Sirjanhaar." p-312

The sakats are deluded; they wander around in the wilderness:

"Saakar bhoola phiray bebaan." p-371

Know the babbling of saakat is like wind passing by:

Saakat ka baknaa ion janau jaisay pavan jholaee." p-609

In this world, the saakats are attached to maya, are miserable and they lose it all at the end of life. In the world beyond- the faithless cynics find no shelter in the Court of the Lord:

"Haltay vich saakat duhelay bha-ay hatho shutak gaiaa.
Agay palat saakat Har dargaah dhoee na paaee." p-734

The faithless cynics have little or no understanding; they do not serve the Lord Har:

"Saakat nar hoshee mutt madham jin Har Har sev naa karaa." p-799

O Nanak the faithless cynics are bound and gagged by the messenger of death and suffer agony in hell:

"Nanak saakat narak maahay jum badhay dukh sahay." p-854

The faithless cynic has to endure 8.4 million hellish incarnations:

"Chaurasee narak saakat bhogeeay." p-1028

If we worship God as energy then the best way to worship and feel God is to go to a power or nuclear plants. To see God close and to become one with Him we should jump into a nuclear blast.

Similarly, if we consider the soul as DNA and, since soul is part of a Infinite God, then God must be an infinite DNA. So it is very easy to see God because DNA, an organic acid, can be seen under a powerful microscope. Since DNA can be altered we ha ave choice to have a designer God.

Calling God as energy is making a mockery of Gurmat.

With regards and prayers for all to be blessed with Gurmat and learn it only from Guru Ji who came to tell us the Truth after seeing the Truth:

"Santan kee sun saachee saakhi.
So boleh jo paikahy aakhee." p-894

MOOL MANTAR

The first line of the Jap Ji- from Ik Ounkar to Gur Parsaad- has been called Mool Mantar in most Sikh literature and declared so by preachers of Sikhi all over the world. But Guru Ji did not call this line Mool Mantar anywhere in SGGS. If this was the Mantar, as generally understood, why is it with different lengths at different places in Gurbani?

The tradition of Mantras has come from Hindu scriptures in which they have thousands of mantras for different wishes or occult powers of which can be obtained by long recitations of these mantras. These powers are called ridh-sidh and can be secured with special practices of these mantras and are still very common among those who want these powers. This is practice by some fake baabaas and other charlatans who want to control others with these powers. But such use is prohibited for Sikhs and Gurbani states so:

"Ridh sidh sabh moh hai Naam na vassay mun aa-ay." p-593

Such special powers are hurdles to spiritual development of one's mind as one can become attached to these powers and thus falls prey to Maya. But are there any Mantras in Gurbani? There are but these are not magic mantras or tantaras but are instead a means, key or method to achieve spiritual development. Here are some Mantras mentioned in Gurbani:

GUR MANTRA

Gur Mantra is a word given by Guru Ji to the Sikh for doing Japna on God's name. Guru Ji uses many names for God that were popular in their era such as Ram, Hari, Gobind, Gopal, Beethla etc. Ram is the most common name used for God in Gurbani. It is not used as the name of Ram avtar but for God. There is no secret word as Gur Mantra in Gurbani, but it is one word to remember God with love and devotion. The formal Gur Mantra for Sikhs is WAHEGURU as mentioned in Gurbani and prescribed by Guru Gobind Singh Ji to Khalsa. Bhai Gurdaas Ji also declares the same in his Vaaran that he got rid of his ego by doing japna on gurmantar Waheguru:

"Waheguru gurmantar hai jap haumay khoee." -Bhai Gurdas

I achieved peace of my mind and with the world outside by doing Naam Japna on Gurmantar:

"Ghar sukh vassia bahar sukh paaia.
Kauh Nanak Gur Mantar dirraaia." p-1136

Life of any person without a Gur Mantra is cursed and contaminated:

"Gur Mantar heenas jo pranee dhrig janam bhrishtanee." p-1356

Here Guru Ji is stressing the need of remembrance of God for a Sikh by accepting a Guru and to receive Mantra from him. Without a Guru, a person is not considered good enough to call his name:

"Nigure kaa hai naaon bura." p-435

BEEJ MANTRA

Beej Mantra is a method of sowing the seeds of Naam in one's mind:

"Beej Mantar Har keertan gaao.

Aagay milay nithanvay thaon." p-891

Beej Mantar is singing the praises of God (reciting Wahe Guru is also singing the praises of God). Even the homeless will find a shelter in Nij Ghar (the spiritual world) after physical death.

SACH MANTARA

Sach Mantar is the means of reaching the True One. Here the Mantra shifts from outward singing, or recitation, of Gur Mantra to listening of a nonstruck melody of Anahad Sabad, God's utterance in inner silence, during sunn. The mind is cleansed by Naam; sabad is Naam and the mind bathes in it to clean itself:

"Oh dhopay Naavay kay rung." p- 4
"Sach Mantar tumara amrit banee.
Seetal Purakh drishat sujani." p-562

Sach Mantar is the listening to the Anhad Sabad (in sunn). So soothing is your presence and the All Knowing gazes at me.

MOOL MANTRA

Mool Mantra is the means or key to knowing the Mool, God. The key/means is only through Naam as Naam is the first creation of God, who created the rest of the universe. Naam is also Sach as Sat Naam and this resides within as Sabad/ Soul. So the return journey for the mind is through Naam which is the direct link to God:

"Appenay aap sajeeo aapeenay rachio Naao." p-463
"Naamay he te Sabh kuch hoa." p-753
"Naam kay dhaaray saglay jant" p-294

As Naam is called Guru/Satguru in Gurbani, then Guru and Satguru are the same as God: "Gur Parmesar eko jaan." So, the real key to God is through Naam. Thus, Guru Ji calls Naam as Mool Mantar; Mool Mantar is the wealth or source of Naam (inside) by which I attained the Perfect Lord:

"Mool Mantar Har Naam rassain kauh Nanak Poora paaia." p-1040

There is a well of Ambrosial Naam inside and through recitation of Gur Sabad I could reach and drink it:

"Anatar koohnta Amrit bhariaa Sabday kaadh peeay panhaari." p-57

These mantras are in line with the progress of spirituality of one's mind as it starts with japna to enter sunn, listening to Sabad there and connecting with Naam which takes one to Sach/Sat/God. No one can achieve liberation without Naam and no one can get Naam without Satguru. God has created such a plan:

"Bin Naavain mukat na paa-vay koee.
Bin Satgur koee Naaon na paa-ay Prabh aisee banat bnaaee hai." p-10

Satguru here is the Sabad Guru inside which one reaches after Naam Japna. He is the immortal Being who is sitting in each one of us:

"Satgur mera sadaa sadaa jo sabh meh rahiaa smaa-ay." p-759

It is through Sabad inside the body that the mind, the live being: jeev, connects with Husband Lord:

"Jeean andar jeeo Sabad hai jit Sauh milaava hoay." p-1250

All these mantras are important markers for one who believes and practices Naam Japna. This is the only means to making a connection with our Mool- God. Improving our behavior in the world is equally important as without virtuous living we cannot do Bhagti or Naam Japna:

"Vin gun keetay bhagt na hoay." p-4

A mind out of control will not cease to think and enter sunn- which is where resides Naam/ Sabad/ Satguru/ Parmatma.

PANCH SHABAD

Panch Shabad in the Anand Sahib and other Banees in the SGGS really refer to the Five Anahad Sounds and not the five Karam Indariyan or five Gian Indaryian. These Shabads and many other Shabads (Vaajey Shabad ghnarey) are not only resounding in the whole universe but also in our body. This is Him, God speaking to His creation and through His creation, but we don't hear it because most of us are deaf to this Anhad Naad. Our ears don't hear it because they have become deaf to spiritual sounds by being clogged up with negative affects of Maya. We don't see His Jot because we are blind to it for the same reason. What we hear is noises from the physical world of Maya:

"Maya dhaaree utt anhaan bola.
Shabad naa sunhi bauh raul ghachola." p-313

In the last pauri of the Anand Sahib, Guru Ji is exhorting us to listen to Anhad Shabad. Only the lucky ones can hear that Shabad. When they hear the Anhad Shabad all their heart's desires will be fulfilled. They will meet Paar Brahm, God in His House, all their sorrow will go away:

"Anhad suno wadbhagio sagal manorath pooray.
Paar Braham Prabh paayaa uttray sagal vissooray." p-917

In every body, God is speaking through and He is the only one speaking:

"Sabhe ghat Raam bole Rama bole.
Raam bina ko boley ray." p-988

Now, how to hear the Sabads? Guru Ji shows us the way to hear these sabads; a prelude to meeting God. The only way to clean up the pollution of the mind is to rid Maya by Naam, through Naam Simran:

"Bhareeay mutt papaan ke sang, oh dhopay Naven ke rung." p-4

Instead of following the advice of Guru Ji, we try to interpret Gurbaani by reading books written by those who have never heard these Sabads and try to explain the meanings in their own limited worldly knowledge. If any person wants to hear these Sabads, it may take more than two months if he does Naam Simran in the company of Gurmukhs. You hear different kinds of sounds like that of chirping birds, school/church bells, sounds of a drum, dancing bells, voilin or a rabaab. After a long practice in Naam Japna and Simrna, the mind is cleansed or becomes pure. The mind has won the Grace of God (Gur Parshaad) and the tenth door opens for that mind for his entry into Nij Ghar. The Panch Shabd will sound together as a welcome back to that lucky mind. These Shabads are listed in one of the hymns on page 884 of SGGS (Kar kar taal pkhavaj naino . . .) and they are: sounds of a Mardang, Rabaab, Flute, Humming Sounds and Dancing Bells. Once the mind has reached home and is ready to meet God in Sehaj Ghar- there is a loud sound of Toor followed by Naad which is another welcome to God's House. It is the duty of every Sikh of Guru Nanak to follow the instructions of Guru as given in SGGS in order to prepare himself for the Anhad Naad to reach Sehaj Ghar:

"Gur kahiaa sa kaar kamaavo
Shabad cheen Sehaj Ghar aavo." p-832

Are we here just to discuss or to do something really good for ourselves and for what we came here for? Please follow SGGS and practice Naam Japna/ Simrna as a basic duty of a Sikh. I will be glad to share any other information from which I gathered in the company of Gursikhs whose only Guru is SGGS.

MIRACLES

A miracle is an occurence that is beyond the comprehension of our intelligence or something that defies any scientific laws. It remains a miracle till we find the cause of such a happening and can repeat it. Then, it is no more a miracle. We cannot say that there are no miracles because now we have come to understand some laws of nature. What we have come to know as nature here is what we know as physically visible to us or our senses. There are some forces in nature which we have been able to recognize, measure, harness and use for our benefit. Their effect on matter and us is no more a miracle. But do we know all the forces in nature? We think we do till we come across some more and are able to understand and utilize these.

This knowledge about the physical matter and forces in nature; electrical, magnetic, gravitational, electromagnetic etc. and the laws that govern these forces that we have derived, is called scientific knowledge. Scientists call these laws the Law of Nature. But these laws relate only to physical matter and the forces that influence this matter and their function under these laws.

Did the Creator Being, God, create only physical nature? Gurbani tells us that He first created Naam, the Creator's Spiritual force, and His extension into the physical world manifested through His utterance called Sabad. It is through Naam, or Sabad, that He created the physical universe and He pervades in each of His creation as Naam. He relishes His creation by sitting within each one of them:

"Aapeenay Aap saajio aapeenay rachio Naaon.
Dooee kudrat saajeeay kar aasan ditho chaao." p-463

There is no difference between God and Soul:

"Atam Ran Ram hai Atam." p-1030

Mind is the subtle physical manifestation of God/Jot inside the body which uses this body for doing its deeds:

"Mun toon Jot saroop hain." p-441
"Tun meh manooa mun meh Sacha." p-686
"Eh mun karma eh mun dharma." p-415

The mind inside the body is called 'jeev' and the body is called 'jant'. The mind is destined to work under Will, or Hukam of God, to conduct its karmas and does all it is required to do:

"Jee jant sabh Tudh upaa-ay.
Jit jit bhaanaa tit tit laa-ay.
Sabh kish keeta tera hoay naheen kish assada jeeo." p-103

So, God's Will acts on our mind through our Soul. So both physical and the spiritual world works under God's Hukam/ Will.

Then there are subtle Mayan forces of three Gunas (Rajgun, Tumgun and Satgun) which influences the mind while it is on a physical journey in the body. When these Mayan forces take over the mind, it loses its identity and becomes a manmukh. A manmukh mind forgets its spiritual origin and identifies itself with the physical body. It fails to recognize spiritual forces Naam/Soul, God and other spiritual creations of God.

The entire spiritual world runs under God's Will and runs, or affects, the physical world under this Will. Once the mind realizes its true self, it becomes like the Soul, or God, and gets the spiritual powers as sanctioned by God. These powers are called the nine Nidhian and eIghteen Sidhian. These are powers that a scientist neither recognises nor understands the effects caused by these powers. So they either call it a miracle or refuse to accept the validity of such occurrence- even when facts speak for itself. These so called miracles are as true as any other occurrence in the physical world but its source, or cause, is spiritual in nature and beyond the comprehension of those who do not recognize these forces or phenomena.

Now let us discuss the Laws of Nature and God's Will:

1. God's Will, or Hukam, is not limited to laws of nature as derived by the scientists due to the fact that these laws do not cover the spiritual field or phenomena. God's Will cannot be defined by us; "Hukam na kahia jaee." His Hukam can be understood only by connecting with Naam. This happens only by the grace of Satguru:

"Eka Naam Hukam hai.
Nanak Satgur deea bujhaay jeeo." p-72

2. God is not bound by the laws of nature which He, Himelf created. He can change these laws whenever He wants or wills. All obey His Will. Nobody is outside His will:

"Hukmay andar sabh ko baahar Hukam na koay." p-1

Whenever He wills, He expands the creation. When He wills, He merges it all into Himself:

"Tis bhaavay ta karay bisthaar.
Tis bhavay ta Ekankar." p-294

All that happens in this world is per Your Will. What can poor man do:

"Jo tis bhaavay so theeay Nanak kiaa manukh." p-417

When He wills, He can keep one alive without breathing:

"Prabh bhaavay bin saas tay rakhay." p -277

3. Man has only been able to understand a tiny bit of His Infinite Creation. He is beyond our comprehension. Rare ones know about Him and those who know about Him cannot dare to say this knowledge:

"Too beant ko virla jaanay." p-562
"Jay haun jaanaa aakhaan naaheen. Kehnaa kathan naa jaaee." p-2

4. To state that scientific Laws of Nature are His Hukam is assuming to know Him and His universe. Perhaps only a Brahmgiaani could try to state this. Even Guru Nanak did not dare to say the he knew God's will.

Conclusion:

Miracles are a reality and happen naturally. Some sidhas do show them to impress others with their miraculous powers- as they did to Guru Nanak in Sidh Gosht. Guru Nanak, however, with the powers bestowed in him did not show any. Although, Gurbani recognizes miraculous powers of ridh and sidh the SGGS does not recommend that one shows off as this will hinder us from achieving and retaining Naam:

"Ridh sidh sabh moh hai Naam naa vassay mun aa-ay." p-583

Because without Naam all food and clothes are worthless; cursed are such spiritual and miraculous powers:

"Bin Naavay painan khaan sab baad hai dhrig sidhi dhrig karmaat."
p-650

The only miracle or spirituality Nanak tells is when Naam comes to abide in the mind of a Gurmukh:

"Nanak Gurmukh Har Naam mun vassay ehaa sidh ehaa kraamaat."
p-650

AKAAL MOORAT

Existence in Mool Mantar is defined by Sat. Parmatama exists as Naam, which is the meaning of Sat Naam. Moorat means the shape or form He takes on in His immanent existence within His creation. His presence within the body is as Naam and He is there in 'sookham moorat':

"Sookham moorat Naam Niranajan kaayaan kaa akaar." p-466

Mind is within the body and within the mind is the True One, God, or His Naam:

"Tun meh munooa mun meh Saachaa." p-686

The Sookham body, which we call subtle body, is within our body that houses His immaculate Naam. This subtle body in which He appears in as Naam is immortal or beyond time. This is what Akaal Moorat means.

God, being beyond time, is covered in Slok "Aad Sach jugad Sach . . ." Time began when the creation came into being. Before that there was no time. God existed in timelessness: "Aad Sach", and exists the same way and will exist in future too.

Sunn, where He exists in transcendental state, is also beyond time. To connect with Him one has to take the mind into sunn, thoughtless state, whether by japna or by following the Guru or any other method which works for the individual:

"Sargun Nirgun Nirankaar sunn samaadhi Aap." p-290

So in brief, Akal Moorat is: the Immortal is the subtle body in which God (as Naam) exists in His creation. Whereas the subtle body in which mind has sheathed itself is made of five components of God's subtle physical creation, Maya, which is not immortal:

"Eh mun panch tutt te janmaa." p-415

This wall, which is linked up with five doots of Maya, has to be continue to make mind pure by linking it with Naam. One must rid it of ego to be worthy of Gurparsad:

"Nanak maya kaa maaran Hari Naam hai." p-513

ASTRAL BODY

The Astral body is the spiritual body most similar to the physical body but is also inside the physical body of each being. It carries the spirit, or soul, of the individual within it. Gurbani calls it 'Sookham Moorat' and it carries the immaculate Naam within it:

"Sookham moorat naam niranjan kaaiaan ka akaar." p-466

Astral body is tied to the physical body at the mool duaar, at a point below the belly-button called 'dharan':

"Mool duaaray baandhiaa bandh." p-1159

Within the astral body resides Naam, the life of the jeev or Atma, and carries the divine light called Jot and which also carries the Anhad Sabad of God:

"Sabh meh Jot Jot hai Soay." p-13
"Sabhay ghat Ram bolay Rama bolay." p-988

Life in the body is because of this astral body which carries the soul and the mind. The mind is the manifestation of God, made up of five subtle basic components of matter/maya. The mind deals with the physical world using the five sense organs of the body and five action organs of the body, and through these does its karma and is also here to do its duty or 'dharma':

"Eh mun karma eh mun dharamaa eh mun panch tutt te junmaa."
p-415

The subtle body lives only on air and has three major arteries for air called Ira, Pingla and Sukhmna which travel from the mool duaar to Trikutee at the center of the forehed just between the eyebrows. This location is also called Third Eye, which is the seat of Siv/God, and mool duaar is the seat of the Sakti/ Maya. Soul plays between these two points called Bhavjal Sagar. God created both these powers of Siv and Sakti and the soul plays between these two under His Hukam:

"Siv Sakat aap upaaykay aapay kartaa hukam vartaay." p-920

God Himself is the Master of these two powers at two ends:

"Doh siriaa kaa aap swaami." p-277

Dasam duaar lies at the trikuti and all spiritual activities involving the crossing of this door takes place in this area and is reflected in the brain. It is often mistaken in the scientific world that the brain is the dasam duaar and all the visions that the mind sees is within the brain activity. Spiritual activity does happen in that area and does affect it but not created by it. Only the spiritual scientists, the true saints, who have experienced this can tell you about this; that is- if you ever consult one.

At death, the astral (or subtle body) leaves the body for good at the command of God. The astral body as, it leaves the body, is called 'huns' or swan. As the swan flies away, the dust of the body mingles with the dust:

"Uddeh huns phurmaaia bhasamay bhasam smaanee." p-1111

When the angel of death opens the knot where subtle body was tied to the physical body and asks the subtle body to leave as per order from God:

"Khulee gunnth uttho likihia aaia Ram." p-1110

Astral body has the same shape as the body and grows inside it. It comes into the mother's womb by the order of the God:

"Saahay kay phurmaaray jee dehi vich jeeo aa-ay paiaa." p-1007

When a seeker on the spiritual of path has acquired enough wealth of Naam, at the third sunn level while in sunn, he or she is blessed to experience the astral travel, leaving the physical body without breaking the knot or tie with the physical body. The link between the physical to the astral body stays through a very fine, subtle thread. The length of travel depends on the amount of spiritual power the mind has been blessed. But the devotee is advised not to travel too far to avoid breaking the link permanently, causing the body to die. The body during this travel remains in smadhi. When one is fully liberated of the maya and achieves union with God, they can then astral travel to the capacity they have. This is how Guru Nanak travelled the universe and wrote about it. He had spiritually seen the universe and found it to be infinite. He could also observe the past and future of the world. He has written about creation of the universe and foretells of the future within the limits of God's Hukam.

I know a few friends in the USA who are doing bhagti and can astral travel. You have to be in sunn smadh. It only indicates that your mind now can temporarily break away from maya but not permanently until you reach the Chautha Pud, which is when you can do it at any time you want- if necessary. There are enough stories about Guru Ji who went to help a devotee at a distant place when the sangat found him asleep. This is the ridh sidh you get but it is given with great responsibility, not to be used to show off and breaking the hukam of the Waheguru. Those who abuse these powers fall back into maya and lose His Grace. Those on the path yet who fall for these powers can never make it to His Grace:

"Ridh sidh sabh moh hai Naam na vasay mun aa-ay." p-593

KEEPING YOUR CHILDREN SIKH

Most Sikh parents living in countries with western cultures expect their children to be Sikhs like themselves, as if they were when in India. They expect them to be obedient, disciplined and respectful to them as they were to their parents. They expect them to be good students, bright and to excel in everything they do. But is this really so? It is true sometimes. We often find that these children look and appear to be obedient but, often, they are only acting to appease their parents into believing what they expect them to be: no dating, no drugs and no moral lapses. They generally stay so in appeasement till they are independent from their parents' support. But sooner or later parents get the shock of their life when their daughter moves out with a non-Sikh boy or their son is found to be taking drugs and never attended the school for which they were paying the fees. They might get another big shock when their teenage child commits suicide due to hiding some guilt, peer pressure or harassment in school due to his turban or long hair. Other very common surprises they get is when their young son, who had been sporting uncut hair till high school or college, comes home having cut his hair, without beard and turban.

Are the parents prepared for all of that? No. Why? They are too busy working and improving their financial situation to improve their social status in the new country they have settled in. Even the mother is busy working, making extra money not only to support the family- but also because she is saving up to buy a new house or to improve their current home. The children are mostly on their own having been raised with the help of baby sitters and TV. When these parents do come home, they are tired and have hardly any time for their children and share very little with them. They expect them to be doing their homework in their rooms. Weekends pass by with these parents doing the chores or shuttling the kids to school games and the evenings are reserved for parties with other Indian friends where the kids are sitting in one corner while the parents are busy gossiping, eating and dancing. Ironically, this is not a party for the kids. So, what we do to offer the kids within our culture or religion? We do very little. Then how do we expect them to be Sikhs? They learn the English language from TV and watch cartoons over the weekends when the parents are busy. So, all that's left for the kids are the teachers, babysitters, cartoons, the internet for all good and bad information and whatever they learned at school and with friends outside the home. At home, they see parents irritated due to being overworked, fighting over things and blaming each other for just about anything and everything. On Sunday, with the parents wanting to be religious, the parents go to Gurdwara and meet other Sikh friends, listen to kirtan or katha, and have a nice meal in the langar hall- which becomes a place for social meeting, a fashion parade and a place to share the latest gossip in town.

During this, what is for the kids? They don't understand anything going on inside the Diwan Hall as everything is done in Punjabi- the language which they don't understand. The program is not designed for their needs. If at the end of the program there is a fight, for whatever reason, kids don't understand it and get totally turned off. They are afraid to go to the Gurdwara when they see violence in a place of worship. They may hate going there next time but the parents will push them to go along with them as they are curious to get an update on the Gurdwara politics and don't want to miss the gossip.

So, if that is our life style in these countries, how do we expect our kids to be Sikhs or good Sikhs? I think we are living in a fool's paradise if we expect that. These kids are being brought up in a land foreign to us, but it is not foreign to them as it is their motherland. So they are exposed, mostly, to the culture of this land- which is very permissive, liberal and independent. At home, they are facing Indian parents who expect them to be like them while they are not doing much about it except feeding them Punjabi food, may be even against their liking. So can we blame our kids, who are not Sikhs, like we expect them to be? No. I think we are expecting way too much while doing way too little about it.

We have a long way to go to raise our kids to be good Sikhs. Question is, are we good Sikhs? Do we know what a good Sikh is supposed to be? In Punjab and India, we did not need to know what this meant as we were living in Sikh culture and imbibed it without studying it. Here, our children don't have that advantage. They are living in a western culture without the aid of grandparents and mother always at home. The first teacher of the child is the mother. It is she who teaches the child the language and Sikh values. Next is the father. The child in the US cannot see much of both of them.

So here are a few recommendations to instill our culture and Sikhi into our children's mind:

1. The parents should become the main role models for the child and live the culture and discipline of Sikhi at home. Due to this, the children will simply just watch their parents and copy them outside of the home. So, the parents should learn about Sikhi and practice it.
2. If you want your children to keep uncut hair, please keep it yourself and teach your children the importance of this as a part of Sikh identity and heritage. Please, go to their school and speak with the teacher and address their class- or ask somebody who can. Explain why Sikhs keep uncut hair, turban, and kirpaan.
3. If you want your children to show love and respect to you, please love them and respect them as well as show love to your spouse. It is the sweet words that keep love alive: "Ganddh preety mithay boal." p-143. It is rude and angry words which break up love: "Tuttee preet gaee bur bol." p-933

4. If you want them to do 'paath' at home, please practice 'paath' home with them sitting next to you, listening and teaching them Gurbani little by little and have them memorize it. Do the 'paath' in the evening and at bedtime as a regular habit. If possible keep one room at home for the Guru Granth Sahib's. Let your children participate in the service and let them do the 'matha teko' in the morning and evening. Do the 'paath' in that room. This will create a special place in their life for Guru Ji. Let them pray for everything in that room to Guru Ji.

5. The best thing you can do for your child is to do Naam Japna with them. They will not only like it- but enjoy it. A child is born after doing Naam Simran in the mother's womb during its stay in there. The only way God keeps the child alive is by taking its mind off the heat in there, "Maat garabh meh apnaa simran deh teh Tum rakhanhaaray." p-613. When born, the child's first cry is for the 'liv'- when the mind is broken from God and not for any pain or hunger. Most of the cries for the first six weeks are due to that separation.

A wise mother will do the japna of Gurmantar, Waheguru, in the child's ears. The child will become quiet right away. They still want to do japna and we don't help them. Rather, we try to connect them with ourselves and after about six weeks- they forget about their link with God. The moh of Maya takes over and now the child cries for the mother or father for toys. "Liv chootee laagee trishnaa maya amar vartaaaia." p-917. Just as Naam Simran saves the baby inside the womb from its heat there, so does it save us from the fire of Maya outside: "Jaisi agan udar meh taisee bahir Maya. Maya agan sabh iko jehi Kartay khel rachaayaa." p-921. If we are blessed, we will continue to feed the child and ourselves with Naam by doing Naam Japna as a regular practice in the morning before we do our 'paath' and in the evening. This guarantees no problems from our children and there will be peace, love and harmony at home. This is the prime duty of a Sikh; "Gur Satgur ka jo Sikh akhaa-ay so bhalkay uth

Hari Naam dhiaay" p-305. This is what distinguishes a Sikh from others.

6. At the community level, we should have a Punjabi school in the Gurdwara where they can learn the language, Sikh history and should also learn to do kirtan. Kids should be allowed to participate in the Sunday program. A special program for the kids should be arranged once a month in English where they do the service: Kirtan, Katha and Ardaas. This will encourage their attendance, learning process and they will be trained to further their participation in the management of the Gurdwara.

7. Do not hesitate to send them to Sikh Camps in the holidays. This way, they will make friends with other Sikhs of their own age and due to this friendship they may end up marrying their own kind.

8. Take them to India to connect them to their roots. They will never forget the hospitality and love they get there.

9. If possible, get your parents over here to stay with you. The kids will learn Punjabi and the Sikh values from them so easily and will love their company.

10. Last but not least, please monitor their use of the Internet. Let the computer be placed in the family room and not in their bed room. This same monitoring should also be done during television time.

Be loving and caring and they will listen to you and develop a trust in you. Your children are the best gifts from God to you. They are your companions in life but are also independent souls. Please treat them as friends. They will be the source of love, joy and hope for the future. They will always love you as you love them. They were also your companions from past lives like your parents, wife, sons, friends, your spiritual master and your brothers. Destiny brings you together again:

"Maat pitaa banitaa sut bandhap isht meet or bhaaee purab janam ke milay sanjogi untay ko na shaee." p-700

SANT, SAADH, BHAGAT
AND BRAHMGIANI

Here is a brief introduction to Sant, Saad, Bhagat and Brahm Giani based in Gurbani.

Sant, Saadh, Bhagat and Brahm Giani are spiritual beings who are self and God realized through their 'bhagti' on Brahm. Their minds are spiritually awakened as they have crossed the 'bhavjal sagar', or the world ocean, and reached the Nij Ghar and Sehaj Ghar. They have become 'jiwan mukat', emancipated while alive, and will not have to be born again as they have no attachments or 'moh' left for the physical world.

They have conquered the five 'doots', evil spirits of Maya, and have achieved the bliss within by uniting with God/Brahm/Parmaatmaa/ Kartaa Purakh/ Ram/Gobind/Hari. Their journey on this planet, which started in Satjug, has come to an end by their worship of God. They have cleansed their mind with Naam through Japna/ Simrna resulting in pure thoughts, words and deeds through blessings of the Guru, and help of True Sants in their spiritual journey back to The Grace of God Who has accepted them back to Its House, Sehaj Ghar. Their minds have reached the 'turiya avastha'/'chautha pad', the spiritual realm.

They are all given a unique assignment from God, or by their own choice, to select one of the four positions to serve Him or revel in the gift of Naam (or dhian, gian as Sants, Saadhs, Bhagats and Brahm

Gianis). These positions are very briefly discussed below on the basis of Gurbani.

SANT

A Sant is assigned the location of where the Anhad Sabad of God goes on all the time. Sant relishes this Anahad Sabad/ Bani/Dhun:

"Teh geet Naad akhaaray sangaa.
Oohaan Bhagat karay Har rangaa." p-739

The Sants have access to the Spiritual wealth of Anhad Bani and holds the key to this. They can help the seeker to this Anhad Sabad:

"Anhad banee poonji.
Santan hath rakhee koonji." p-893

Sants will brief the seekers on 'akath katha', the invisible path to reach the Supreme Being. This is their assignment:

"Kahaiy Nanak suno santo kathio akath khanee." p-918

Through this anhad bani, which God Himself is uttering inside every human, will reveal this unknown path to the seeker when they hear it under the guidance and help of a Sant:

"Har ki katha Anahad Bani." p-439

Sants become servants of God and have easy access to His mansion. They know well their Divine Master and will guide the seeker to Him:

"Pucho ja-ay pdhaaooaan chalay chaakar ho-ay. Rajan jaa-nay aapnaa dar ghar thaak na hoay." p-57

The Sants are directed by God to do simran on Gurmantra above everything else and help others to do the same to bring peace to them:

"Saajan Sant karo eh kaam. Aan tiaag jappo Har Naam.
Simar simar sukh paavo. Aap jappo avray Naam japaavoh." p-290

SAADHU

Saadhus are blessed with doing 'kirtan', singing praises of Naam and the True One. The Sadhus will deliver this 'kirtan' to those who accept Guru's word as Truth:

"Ram Naam kirtan rattan vath Saadhu paas rakheejay.
Jo bachan Gur sat sat kar ma-nay tis aa-gay kaadh dhreejaiy." p-1326

Since Sehaj Dhun goes on with Naam, Saadhus stay with Sehaj Dhun. If we keep the company of Saadhus and renouncing the ego beg for help- they will help us cross the Bhavjal/ Agan Sagar by bringing us to the treasure of Naam:

"Aap shod benati karoh.
Saadh sang agan sagar taro." p-295

If we desire the Four Cardinal Gifts, we should go and serve Sadhus:

"Chaar pdarath je ko maangay.
Saadh janaa kee sewa laagay." p-266

Meeting our True Lord is the only purpose of this human birth. One is advised that the only important thing in life is to do Japna in the company of a Saadh:

"Bhaee parapt manukh dehuria. Gobind milan kee ehi teri baria. Avar kaaj teray kitay naa kaam. Mil sadh sangat bhaj kewal Naam." p-12

BHAGAT

Bhagat stays in high comfortable spiritual palaces of Sookh Mehal:

"Sookh mehal jaa kay ooch dwaaray.
Taa meh vassay bhagat piaaray." p-739

Bhagats are always imbued with the peace of God's Naam:

"Sukhmani sukh amrit Prabh Naam.
Bhagat janaa kay mun bisraam." p262

Bhagat's food for mind is only Hari Naam and they are always heard singing praises of God. They live in the Nij Ghar serving God and win respect at the door of His Mansion:

"Bhagtan ka bhojan Hari Naam Niranjan pehnan bhagat bdaaee. Nij Ghar vaasa sadaa Har sewan Har Dar sobhaa paaee." p-1233

In the Japji Sahib, Guru Ji has dedicated four pauries to Bhagats. They are always in peace and happiness and listening to them many-a-grief and sins are dispelled:

"Nanak Bhagtan sadaa vigaas.
Sunniay dookh paap ka naas." p-2

God loves His Bhagats and they look beautiful singing His praises at His door:

"Bhagat teray mun bhaanvday.
Dar sohan keertan gaanvday." p-262

BRAHM GIANI

Brahm Giani is a seeker whose mind is fully awakened into the spiritual realm and lives in Sach Ghar, having gained independence from doots of Maya. He is liberated from the cycle of reincarnations:

"Sache mehal niwaas nirantar aavan jaan chukaaia." p-7

Food for his mind is Brahm Gian, or the knowledge of the Infinite Being. His mind, at all times, absorbed in deep meditation of Supreme Lord:

"Brahngiani ka bhojan giaan.
Nanak Brahm Giaani ka Brahm dhiaan." p-273

No diffence is there in the nature of God and Brahm Giani:

"Nanak Brahm Giani aap Parmesar." p-273

They are, most of the time, in deep meditation and serve God in simran in that state only. Brahmgiani's mind is always in self control and remains pure:

"Nadri Satgur seveeay nadri sewa hoay.
Nadari eh mun vas aavay nadri mun nirmal ho-ay." p-558

TRUE SANTS AND SADHUS

With the mere mention of Sant or Sadhu, we start condemning them as Baabaas or Deraawaalaas. Fake Babaas and Deraawaalaas have given a bad name to the True Sants and Sadhus who are mentioned in Gurbani, again and again. It is in our ignorance, without understanding Gurbani, that we feel no need of the true ones whose job it is to help us on this path of our spiritual progress to unite with our Maker, the Nirankar. Since most of us are not on that path of truly seeking Him, but busy in our own worldly affairs seeking wealth, name and fame- we never feel the need of such saintly people and so are happy in our own pursuits. But, ask a seeker who can not meet and see Parmatma and is crying for help. Is there a friend who can release me from my bondage (of maya) and unite me with God, recite His Name to me and make this mind stable and steady, so that it no longer wanders around?:

"Bandhan te chuttkaavay Prabhu milaavay Har Har Naam sunaavay.
Asthir kray nehchal eh manooaa bauhar naa kabhoo dhaavay." p-674

Do I have such a friend? I would give him all my property, my mind, my heart and my consciousness:

"Hai koee aiso hamraa meet.
Sagal smagri jeeo heeo deon arpon apnaa cheet." p-674

Guru Ji then gives the answers to the above question, as to what one should do if one desires to meet with God with such intensity. Give up your love for other's wealth, other's property and the slander of others. Associate with the True Saints and keep your mind tuned to the singing of Lord's praises and your mind will awaken to spiritual reality:

"Par dhan par tun par ki nindaa in sio preet na laagay.
Santah sung sant sanbhakhan Har keertan mun jaagay." p-674

God is the treasure of virtues, kind, compassionate and the source of all comforts. Nanak begs the gift of Naam, from You O Lord, like a child asks from mother and father:

"Gun nidhaan dayal Purakh Prabh sarab sookh dyaalaa.
Mangay daan Naam tero Nanak jion maat pitaa Gopaalaa." p-674

True Sants and Sadhus are not our Gurus, but helpers and guides on this spiritual path about which Gurbani is mentioning, again and again. These Sants and Sadhus have made union with God with the help from other Gurmukhs, Satguru and God Himself and are here to help us. This guidance and help is necessary because it is not easy for us to understand the practical difficulties that one comes across while traveling on this spiritual path where our object of love, our mind and the Satguru sitting inside us are all invisible. And so are the five doots of Maya which are the major hindrance on this path. The struggle of the mind is with them and they do not let our mind alone and, instead, keeps it busy with some thought, or other, related to the three gunas of Maya. The main battle is to fight them so that we still the mind, and that is where Naam Japna comes in. At the same time, we have to be truthful in our words, deeds and thoughts. We all have to work together towards that goal. Sants and Sadhus guide, advise and help us on the path till we are united with our source, Nirankar. Without them it is not possible to make it unless God Himself comes and pulls us out of this bhavjal sagar. Below are some quotes from Gurbani to understand the need of such a help on the path.

The sole purpose of the coming of a Sant is that in his company, Naam is meditated on:

"Jan aavan ka ehai suaao.
Jan kay sang chit aavay Naao." p-295

It is only through the help of a Sadhu that one can meet God:

"Sadhu sangat hoay praapat ta Prabh apnaa laeeay." p-713

It is in the company of a Sadhu that I understood how to get Naam:

"Sadhu sang sikhaaio Naam." p-393

Meditate on the Name of God in the company of a Saadhu:
"Sadhu sang bhajo Gopal." p-275

With God's grace one gets the company of a Saadhu. The more we have such company, the more we get closer to God:

"Kirpa karay jis Paarbrahm hovay Sadhu sang. Jio Jio oh vdhaeeay tio tio Har sio rang." p-204

Because of my past good deeds I met a Saint. In his company, I met God and all my spiritual darkness vanished and my mind woke up from sleep (under Maya) of many-a-past lives:

"Purab karam unkar jab pragtay bhetio purakh rasik bairaagi. Mittio andher milat Har Nanak janam janam ki soee jagee." p-204

Becacuse of my good fortune, Guru made me meet a Sant who helped me realise God within my own body:

"Bhaag hoa Gur Sant milaaia.
Prabh abinaasee ghar meh paaia." p-97

In the company of saints I got liberation from the cycle of births and deaths:

"Nanak Sadhu sang janam maran swaaira." p-854

Whosoever sought company of a Sadhu, he is emancipated from this world (bhavjal sagar) and his mind enters the Chautha Pad (Paargraam):

"Jo jo saran paray Sadhu kee so pargramee keea." p-610

Both Saint and God need to be served. God is the provider of liberation and the Sant makes us do Naam japna to be worthy of that:

"Kabir sewa ko doo-au bhalay ek Sant ik Ram.
Ram jo daataa mukat ka Sant jpaa-vaiy Naam." p-1373

Take pity on me O Lord of the World, O Great Giver, let me fall on the feet of the Saints. I will cut my head and cut it into small pieces, O Nanak, for the Saints to walk upon:

"Mo kau dhaar kirpaa Jag Jeevan Daatay Har Sant pagee leh paavay. Hau kaaton kaat baadh sir raakhaun jit Nanak Sant charh aa-vay." p-881

There are hundreds of quotes in Gurbani telling us the need of a true Saint/ Saadhu to help us achieve the goal in human life of uniting with God and winning emancipation to live in bliss. Just because there are some fake ones around, we may have to be careful in finding the true ones who have no other mission in life but to help people unite with God through Naam Japna, and giving guidance on the path through doing 'akath katha'. A Saadhu helps us overcome our separation from God and helps us realize our plan of becoming one with Him on this planet to reach our true home. A true saint will ask for nothing in return for this service as this is his assignment from whom He serves, God, Who has already rewarded bliss to him.

The fake Sant will be collecting 'bheta' and ask for funds for his own projects in progress at his 'dera'. Their katha will be derived from history and stories- but not on spirituality, will never discuss akath katha and will do keertan on 'kachi banee'. He will promise to fix all worldly problems through his special powers, prayers and akhand paths etc. He will seek name and fame and will advertise his visits, as well as want to meet all his admirers and visit their homes in order to bless them. He will have good links with politicians who depend on him for votes. Whereas, the True Sant will not ask or promise anything but will, instead, bless the person to start Naam Japna and acceptance to the Hukam of God as all is happening in His Hukam. The fake ones are known all over the world, whereas the True ones you will have to search or beg God in order to connect you with them.

KHALSA REHAT AND SCIENCE

The word Khalsa and its history belong to kings, whether of land or army. Again, in Sikh history, it has been used by Guru Ji for the sangat to report to Guru Ji, instead of the masands. After that, Guru Gobind Singh Ji's wife used Khalsa to refer to the Sangat and thereafter, the Khalsa sangat used it for other members of the Sikh sangat. It is very well known that all the followers of the Gurus did not take Khanday Di Pauhal and had Hindu and Muslim names but were members of the Sikh army which later came to be known as the Khalsa sangat. But, was there another Khalsa which Guru Gobind Singh Ji created after the new initiation ceremony? Yes. There was also the Khalsa sangat of Guru Ji but there is a big difference. This Khalsa Guru Ji created belonged to Waheguru:

"WAHEGURU JI KA KHALSA" -Sarab Loh

Guru Nanak had envisioned this Khalsa and created it in the tenth form- the ideal man whose duty to save the lives and liberty of people that cried for help. This Khalsa is the army of God and evolved at the desire of God, The Akal Purakh:

"KHALSA AKAAL PURAKH KI FAUJ.
PARGATTIO KHALSA PARMAATAM KI MAUJ." -Sarab Loh

This Khalsa is Sant-Siphai, the Saint-Soldier. Guru Ji infused in them a new spirit of a fearless warrior: one who would fight for truth and justice, one who not only protected himself but also the weak, oppressed and saintly people from tyrant rulers- destroying these tyrants from their very roots. His duty is to let people know their true responsibility as a human. Let all saintly people understand this:

"Yahee kaaj dhara hum junmum, samajh leeo sadhu sabh mumum. Dharam chalaavan sant ubhaaran, dushat sabhan ko mool upaaran." -Chaupaee Bachitttar Natak

And, so, the Sikhs of the Guru became Khalsa after taking the 'Khanday Di Pauhal'. This became the initiation for all Sikhs to pledge their allegiance to their new brotherhood of Khalsa, which stood for the liberty and freedom of the people. Every Sikh's first duty as a Sikh was to take Khanday Di Pauhal. Only the initiated Sikhs commanded more respect among the Sikhs:

"Pratham rehat yeh jaan Khanday kee pauhal chhakay.
Soee Singh pardhaan avar naa pauhal jo layay." -Rehatnaama Bhaee Desa SIngh

When we follow the discipline (rehat) as ordered by the Guru, we will be considered a Sikh of the Guru. Then Guru will honor him as his master and himself as his disciple:

"Rehani rhay soee Sikh mera.
O Sahib meh us ka chera." -Rehatnaama Bhaee Desa Singh

FIVE Ks and REHAT

It is wrong to assume that the Sikhs started wearing 5ks at the order of Guru Gobind Singh Ji. They started keeping this rehat under earlier Gurus. They started wearing Kirpan at the instance of Guru Hargobind Ji. Guru Gobind Singh Ji only altered the ceremony to Khanday Di Pauhal and made the five 5ks compulsory for all initiated Sikhs.

Five Ks are mentioned in Rehatnaamas of Bhaee Nand Lal Ji and other Rehatnamas of Sikhs of the Guru during Guru's time and beyond. Guru Ji told all the Sikhs coming to the Sangat not to show their face to the Guru without hair and wearing kirpan:

"Eh meri aagiaa suno re piaaray.
Bina teg kesun divay na deedary." -Rehatnama Bhaee Desa Singh

Guru Ji declared Sikhs without arms and kes as sheep:

"Binaa sastar keson nrun bhed jaano." -Rehatnama Bhaee Sukha Singh, Gur Bilaas

A Sikh of the Guru was to comb the hair twice a day and tie the turban afresh:

"Kungha dono vakat kar paag chunaiy kar bandhaee." -Bhai Nand Lal Ji

A gursikh was to get up early morning with love and devotion in his heart and do jaap of Gurmantar, Waheguru. After their bath, they were to recite Japji and Jaap. In the evening, he was to listen to Reharaas and glories of God in Keertan and Katha:

"Gursikh rehat suno hay meet, parbhaatay uth kar Har cheet.
Waheguru gurmantar su jaap, kar isnaan parhay Jap jaap.
Sandhya samain sunay rehraas, kirtan kathaa sunay Har yas." -Bhai Nand Lal

A present day Panthic Sikh Rehat Maryada is based on all the different rehatnamas written at the time of Guru Ji and the time of later Sikhs. This was approved by Khalsa Panth with the seal of Akal Takhat. This is the Rehat, or discipline, for all Sikhs and its purpose is to guide us on all aspects of the temporal life of the Sikhs at the individual and societal level, whereas, Gurbani of the Sri Guru Granth Sahib elaborates on our spiritual source and how to achieve our spiritual goals to realize ourselves and to connect with our Source, Parmatama, through Naam. Gurbani fully guides the seeker to the spiritual goal, whereas, SRM gives basic guidelines for how to live our life as Sikhs. Both are equally important for a Sikh to live a successful life.

KHALSA and SCIENCE

Sikh religion is not based on somebody's philosophy but on Gurmat as it came to our Gurus and Bhagats direct from the Source. Its spiritual contents, like that of any other religion, cannot be scientifically tested or verified as it deals with our inner spirit and God, who and which are not material. Science, however, deals only with the physical part of God's world and it is based on the understanding of matter which can be tested and evaluated to comprehend intellectually and to convince others by the physical presence of proof. In religion and spirituality, the only way to verify the claims is to live life as the Guru stated and to experience the proof within your own inner self. If someone wants to see or experience God, they can do so by following the Guru's instructions:

"Grubani khay sewak jan maanay partakh Guru nistaaray." p-972
"Nanak ka Patshah disay zahraa." p-1096

Sikhism is a religion full of hope and promise by the Satguru provided Sikhs follow the Guru. Here, Guru Ji is telling our mind that it will gain happiness serving the Satguru, Waheguru. All your desires will be fulfilled and you will suffer from no grief:

"Meray mun Satgur sev sukh hoee.
Jo isho soee fal paavo phir dookh naa viaapay koee." p-882

Now how to serve Satguru or Har is to do Japna on His Name:

"Har kee tehal kmaavani japeeay Har kaa Naam." p-300

There is a challenge facing scientific minded people who want proof. Please do the Naam Japna and find out the truth of Gurbani. If you do not want to do Naam Japna, do not call the Sikh religion a wishy washy religion lost in a maze of rituals. May be Naam Japna/Naam Simran looks like a useless ritual to scientific people. If you are a scientist, please try it out like a scientist under the guidelines of Gurbani and then make a statement. Please do not reject it without even testing Naam Simran as it is the most unscientific thing you can practice. Guru Ji had eliminated the priestly class. It is us who wanted the priests back in order for them to teach us. The preists are only there to make money and will even create rituals in order to do this. We do not want to learn Gurbani, but will pay others to serve the Satguru. This is the worst insult to the Guru. Sikhism teaches of sacrificing one's body, mind and breaths (in sunn) to the Guru and to accept His Will to reach Him:

"Tun mun dhan sabh saunp Gur kau Hukam maneeay paaeeay." p-918

We do not even have the time for the Guru but blame other Sikhs, Sikh history and denounce genuine Sikh scholars who spent their life time studying and writing about Gurus and Gurbani. We are critics, agnostics and cynics lost in our own maze of intellectual distortion of Gurbani, Sikh history and traditions- looking at them with an eye of a harsh intellectual for our own ego. Our ego cannot judge spiritual values whether it is the 5ks, Naam or Naam Japna etc.

If you do not believe in the Soul, how can you believe in God? The Soul is God within each one of His creations. We can keep talking about how to live a good ethical life but that is only humanism which is another name for atheism. These critics condem false sants, deraawaalaas, but they are intellectual deraawaalaas who do not understand Guru's spiritual message and keep twisting this message to confuse innocent and ignorant Sikhs who had never had a chance to read Gurbani before. So, if something does not appeal to our intellect, we should bring it up in this forum for discussion rather than finding faults with it even if it is part of Gurbani.

KHALSA - WAHEGURU'S OWN

Every Sikh is required to take Khande De Pauhal when he/she comes of age and can handle the discipline as prescribed in Sikh Rehat Maryada (SRM). For this, it is essential for every Sikh to believe in and follow the SRM as prepared by Guru Panth and ordered by Akaal Takhat. This is supposed to be the first requirement for a Sikh and thus only baptized Sikhs will be respected among the Sikhs:

"Pratham Rehat yeh jaan Khanday kee pauhal chhakay.
Soee Singh pardhaan avar naa pauhal jo la-ay." -Rehatnama Bhaee Desa Singh

Whoever follows the discipline (rehat), as ordered by the Guru, will be considered a Sikh of the Guru and he will honor them as his equal. One should not call himself a Sikh without following the prescribed discipline. Without the discipline, life will result in wandering and suffering. Without the discipline, one will never find peace within and it is for this very reason that a Sikh should strictly follow the Sikh discipline (rehat):

"Rehani rahay soee Sikh mera. O Sahib mein us ka chera.
Rehat bina naheen Sikh kahaavay. Rehat bina dar chottan khaavay.
Rehat binaan sukh kabhoo naa layay. Taan tay rehat so drid kar rahay." -Rehatnama Bhaee Desa Singh

Guru Gobind Singh Ji, himself, did not write any rehatnaamaa but they were written by Sikhs during Guru Ji's time who had witnessed events and later on by others who had received the information by word of mouth and from their own observation of the practice, which continued from the time of the Guru Ji. We cannot discard it as non-authentic because it is not written by Guru Ji. Even Bhai Nand Lal Ji wrote on Rehat. Gurus came to instruct us on spiritual discipline for the spiritual awakening of our mind and they did write what we call Gurbani. However, Guru Gobind Singh Ji did define Khalsa in one of his swayaa given below:

KHALSA is the one:

Who focuses his mind on the Light of God within Himself day and night and never swerves from the thought of One God; who has full confidence and love for God and does not put his faith even by mistake in fasting, graves, crematoriums and jogi's place of sepulcher; who does not believe in pilgrimages, giving alms, penance and austerities but believes only in one God; whose heart is lit with the Light of God, such a Khlasa is considered to be the Pure one:

"Jagat Jot japaiy nis baasar, Ek bina mun naik naa aanaiy.
Pooran prem parteet sajaiy brat, gor marhee mutt bhool naa jaanaiy.
Teerath daan dayaa tup sanjam, Ek binaa neh Ek pechhanaiy.
Pooran Jot jagaiy ghat me, tub Khalsa taahay nikhaalas jaanaiy."
-Guru Gobind Singh 33 Swayay

Again Guru Ji declared Khalsa as the one who receives the Spiritual Nectar of Naam in their heart. And hence Guru Ji says that there is no difference between God Almighty, the Guru himself and the Khalsa thus created:

"Atam rus je janaee so hai Khaalsaa dev.
Prabh meh mo meh taas meh ranchak nahin bhev." -Sarab Loh

Guru Ji promised that so long as Khalsa maintains its spiritual purity, he will bestow all his blessings on him. But when the Khalsa abandons the spiritual path, adopting the ritualistic Brahminical ways, he will stop caring for them:

"Jab lug Khalsa rahe niaara. Tub lug tej dioon meh saaraa.
Jab eh gahe bipran ki reet. Meh naa karon in ki parteet." -Sarab Loh

Guru Ji was in so much awe at the vision of Khalsa that he could not help praising Khalsa:

'If all cells of my body would become tongues, I would praise Khalsa with all those tongues. He belonged to the Khalsa and that Khalsa and him were just like drops of water in one ocean':

"Rome rome je rasnaa paaon, tabat Khalsa jas haun gaaoon.
Haun Khalse ko Khalsa mero oatpoat sagar boondero." -Sarab Loh

Guru Ji says he enjoyed his exalted position, owing to the Khalsa; otherwise there were plenty of ordinary men like him:

"Inhi ki kirpa ke saje hum hain. Nahin mo so gareeb krore paray."
-Gian Parbodh

Guru Ji says that he won all the battles because of Khalsa, and because of Khalsa he had been able to serve humanity:

"Judh jite inhee kay parsad. Inhee kay parsaad so daan kare." -Gian Parbodh

Guru Ji infused in them a new spirit of a fearless warrior, who would fight for truth and justice; one who could not only defend himself, but also protect the weak, the oppressed and other saintly people from the tyranny of the rulers. Guru Ji says he was born for this express purpose and let all the saintly people understand this:

"Yahee kaaj dharaa hum janmum.
Samajh leo saadhu sabh munmum.

Dharam chlavan sant ubaaran.

Dushat sabhan ko mool upaaran." -Chaupaee Bachittar Natak

The Khalsa, declared by Guru Ji during his time after having his followers take the Khande Dee Pauhal, had the spiritual status as described above. Do we, who take the Khande Dee Pauhal now, have our spiritual level anywhere near to the definition of Khalsa given by Guru Ji? A Khalsa is supposed to be a Saint- Soldier. It appears we are neither saints nor soldiers, but some of us do put the title of Khalsa after our name. We should seriously think about it before we take such a title.

Khande Dee Pauhal now has just become a ceremony to make a commitment of our discipline to the Guru and to prepare to be a saint and soldier. To become a true Khalsa we have to become saints, the ones within whom the Light of God shines with constant awareness of God's presence, in mind. If we do not meet the above criteria, we better prepare ourselves for that before we call ourselves a Khalsa.

Getting baptized by the Panj Piaray who have not given their head to the Guru (those who have fully surrendered their lives to the Guru/God and are lit with the Light of Naam) cannot yet instill that kind of spirituality within us. Neither, are we prepared, ourselves, to be a Saint ready for Amrit- the real nectar which comes from within after taking it from the Pure Panj Piaray. But that should not discourage from taking Khande Dee Pauhal as it is a good place to start the journey toward that end as we delve into Sikh discipline. With the grace of Guru and Waheguru, we will one day be ready for the ultimate state of Pure Khalsa and be one with God in order to win respect as a Waheguru Ji ka Khalsa and be ever ready to fight for the cause of Truth and Justice under His command by being a member of the 'Akal Purakh kee Fauj'.

I am wishing you all a very happy Birthday of The Khalsa, an ideal being envisioned by Guru Nanak, which took nearly two centuries of preparation to evolve. Who finally brought hopes of people to be free to a reality when they secured their own land into a self-rule of peace and security. To win such a situation back we have to become pure Khalsa again. Let us pledge to prepare for that goal to live in peace, prosperity and dignity.

HEAVEN AND HELL

Heaven and Hell are two places about which everybody is concerned with. They are afraid to go to hell because they will suffer, but prefer heaven as a better place to live. Guru Granth Shhib states that God is within the human body and all around in the universe. A person's soul shuttles between trikuti (confluence of Ida, Pingla and Sukhmana, air vessels of sookham body, between two eyebrows) and mool-duaar (an inch below the naval point and an inch inside the stomach). A person's mind only has to travel from mool-duaar to tri-kuttee after death. Gurmukhs go straight to Trikutti (Nij Ghar), the seat of God, because they had gained direct access to Nij Ghar when alive. They do not have to meet jumdoot and Dharam Raj as they directly go to Nij Ghar and are treated with respect there as a free person. A Manmukh, however, has to be pulled out of his body by jumdoot when he comes at the last breath of the body and breaks the knot of sookham body at the mool duaar. The person gets scared of jumdot and runs away but jumdoot, a scary being, catches the person and hits him on the head to wake the person's mind from sleeping under Maya. This person feels sorry for what he did during his life (under Maya) but now it is too late. He calls his relatives but nobody comes there to help him. He is insulted and squeezed, like in oil press, and tortured, like he is in flames. He is judged at the Dhram Raj Court and the case is presented to God- Who writes his destiny according to what he did in this life on earth. God then lets him be born into a suitable family where he can learn more about his/her goal.

In fact, there is no place like heaven or hell in Sikhism. Dead people in their astral body live in the air in the atmosphere and wait for their next birth. The Gurmukh lands up straight in Nij Ghar because of his past travels to Nij Ghar while alive. He is greeted by God and enjoys peace and bliss there. He is free from the birth and death cycle. The manmukh's destiny and specie level is written for the next life by God. He is fully awake now and has to bear the mental agony of all the punishment given to him. He is further punished with the cycle of reincarnation and may go through repeated miscarriages. Manmukhs get birthed right away because there are plenty of manmukh parents of the right specie level decided because of his karmas. A manmukh person will not get his next life as human, but those who have done some naam japna during life time will get human birth. That person will find parents with more difficulty, but a near-gurmukh finds parents with even more difficulty as there are very few parents around who are suitable for him.

Persons who are stuck at the third sunn and could not move upward become angels. They do not have to born again. They live in a space in the sky where they float around in their astral bodies supported by air only. They had done enough bhagti in their time on earth but were not successful in meeting God. They live in Maya in the sky. They could not complete their journey to God when they were alive. They soon get tired of this leisurely life and pray to God for human birth in order to do more bhagti to achieve salvation in their life time and to meet God. When their prayer is heard, their astral body waits in the sky till the right parents are found. When born again, they may find holy company to do enough bhagti in order to be accepted by God to let them into Nij Ghar when their journy on earth ends.

To obtain the state of liberation of Nirvana meditate on One True Lord:

"Jivan pud nirbaan Iko simreeay." p-232

One who keeps Naam in his heart is Jiwan-Mukt, liberated while alive: "Jis Naam ride so Jiwan-Mukta." p-1156

So perform good deeds and chant the Gurmantra, you will never have to go to hell:

"Sukrat kareeay Naam leejay narak mool na jaaeeay." p-705

Kabeer, I have been spared from hell and heaven by the grace of True Guru:

"Kabeer surag narak te meh rahio Satgur ke parsad." p-1370

If you are involved only in Maya, you are bound to go to hell:

"Narak surag avtar Maya dhandian." p-676

So, the best thing to do is to achieve salvation in this life and to live in peace during this life in order to never to be born again. What happens after death is explained in detail in four essays on 'Death and After' in this book at the end. Readers are expected to read those essays for further information.

DISCUSSIONS ON GURMAT

Discussion on Gurmat is supposed to help us understand Guru's teachings, which are given in Gurbani. For that, one has to learn and understand what Guru Ji is saying about the subject under discussion in Gurbani. So, one has to read Gurbani and comprehend it or read about the subject from books of renowned scholars of Gurbani in English or Punjabi. Trying to grasp Gurbani and asking about or quoting the Gurbani in discussion, for further clarification, helps others understand it better. But, the ultimate authority on Gurmat is Gurbani, itself. When we are not sure about the meaning of a sentence or a word in Gurbani, it is best to look up the translations in English or Punjabi and to try to put the meaning of it together to see if the translation fits with the rest of the teachings of the Shabad. If it is not clear, one should not hesitate to ask someone in the forum.

However, to quote your own ideas about the subject without knowing what Guru Ji is saying regarding the subject is not Gurmat discussion, but purely an intellectual debate or pushing your own ideas about Gurmat on to others. Our own ideas about life, the purpose of life, death, and life after death may not match Gurmat, but we believe in it so strongly that we try to push it onto others without quoting or misquoting Gurbani. That does not make it Gurmat discussion. There are so many scholars on religion and spirituality that may sound very convincing to us and some of us may quote them without checking if their ideas match Gurmat. There are so many books written by atheists and agnostics, which will be very persuasive to our logical and scientific minds, but should you push those ideas as Gurmat or misinterpret Gurbani to match those ideas? It will be totally anti- Gurmat.

Some times, we may misinterpret some Gurbani words as it may suit our belief system and we may push these understandings onto others- this is not fair, either. Sometimes we will look up quotes which appear to match our beliefs and quote it without caring in what context Guru Ji had said it- we could be wrong there, as well. Until we have complete understanding of Gurmat and the Game of life, which Guru Ji calls Akath Katha and really means 'story of our spiritual journey to meet Akal Purakh', we will not be able to interpret Gurbani correctly. This knowledge does not come from reading books or just reading Gurbani even though it tells about it- we won't understand it as it is beyond our intellectual grasp, belonging to the spiritual arena. It will have to come from Sabad Guru, who sits inside us, and gives us the Spiritual Knowledge when we are in touch with Him inside. The only way to meet with Sabad Guru is to go where he is:

"Satgur mera sadaa sadaa na aavay na jaa-ay." p-308

Guru Ji tells us again and again to connect with Sabad Guru with the help of those who have gone over the journey and know it very well. Guru Ji calls them Sants, Sadhus, Bhagats, Brahmgianis and Gurmukhs. But, not having read or understood Gurbani correctly, we don't understand the need of them or identify them. It is just like we are trying to become a doctor just by reading books on medicine without going to medical school or without the help of other doctors who are experts in the field. We will be total failures, confused and and will confuse, misguide and hurt others.

SRM is a practical guide for a Sikh as to how to live their life in the day-to-day world and prepare them for their spiritual development. Naam Japna in the morning is one of the basic duties of a Sikh. But how many believe in it, do it or know how to do it? Being truthful in thoughts, words and deeds is a basic requirement to prepare for Naam Japna, or Bhagti Karni, but is not an end in itself. But, most of us are stuck there. We can become Satguni but that is still living in Maya. We have to cross over the Bhavjal Sagar. For that, we have to connect with Sabad Guru by going inside with the help of Naam Japna but we don't believe in or practice on it. So how will that help us?

So sitting in Satgun full of ego of being there, we are stuck there. If we gain a little bit of knowledge we think we are better than all and become judge on everything others say. It takes us nowhere. Most of the discussions in the forum on Gurmat are based at intellectual plane and can lead us nowhere when the goal is spiritual. We repeat the same subject over and over again but still stick to the same views we had before discussion as the correct answer doesn't appeal to our intellect. We call ourselves scientific, but we do not apply any scientific means to evaluate the principle of spirituality as Guru Ji recommends. So, we reject most of the spiritual principles and many basic doctrines as we fail to understand them and hence don't believe in them.

It is not easy to give up our munmatt and adopt Gurmatt. But without doing that we will not get Gurmat. The only way Guru Ji recommends to do is through regular Naam Japna which will connect us to Satguru, the Sabad Guru, who will give us Gurmatt:

"Mun ki matt tiaago harjan ehaa batt kathaini.
Andin Har Har Naam dhiaavo Gur Satgur ki matt laini." p-209

The spiritual knowledge will come along with that from Satguru, himself, and all the ignorance and spiritual darkness will vanish:

"Giaan anjan Gur deea agiaan andher binaas." p-293

With the Grace of God, I met a True Saint with whose help my mind, says Nanak, got illumined with Divine Light:

"Har kirpa te Sant bhetia Nanak mun pargas." p-293

I hope that these basic guidelines will help make the Gurmat discussions more fruitful.

RELIGION SCIENCE AND GURMAT DISCUSSIONS

For the last few centuries, there has been a lot of study of physical nature called science which provides a deeper insight into nature, an understanding about how various forces in nature operate and then scientific laws were developed about these forces called laws of science. These laws relate to forces; gravitational, motion, hydraulic, electrical, chemical, thermodynamic etc. Based on the understanding of all this and deeper study of the matter, itself, has resulted in development of machines, tools, equipment which has made our day-to-day life very convenient in letting us achieve far more with our labor and time as compared to a couple of centuries ago. We can now live in greater comfort at home or our place of work with this controlled environment. We can communicate much faster with the help of new telephones, the internet and travel at speed of sound etc. The new discoveries have helped usher in different phases of our life on this planet.

The emphasis, now, on education has shifted from religious and spiritual studies to physical sciences which bring us better employment with more comforts in life. People now feel better protected from forces of Nature and feel less dependent on God and gods, notwithstanding the fact that natural calamities still occur- though we have better means of sending help and saving some lives. With better and faster means of transportation, business has become global but more complicated, dependent on stock markets and more risky economies world-wide. With all the conveniences, an average man has become far more busy and worried than ever before resulting in heavy stress on the mind and body. Industrialization has polluted air, water and ground resulting in many more diseases and physical ailments. The fear of the wrath of God and gods has been replaced by global warming, resulting in rising of sea waters on ground and the fear of nuclear war which can result in the annihilation of humanity. A simple, carefree life has become far more complicated with almost no help from the elders of our family as the family unit has become broken and divorces are common. Natural healing methods developed over millenniums have been replaced by chemical drugs which only suppress symptoms and cause side effects which are as dangerous as the disease itself.

Life on this planet has turned into a far more complicated drama where man is trying to depend only on his own intellect and has been giving up faith in God and spirituality. People are turning from being a theist to atheist and giving it the socially acceptable name of being a secular humanist. The search within has turned to the search outside for peace and happiness, which lies within all of us: "Sukh sagar Hari Naam hai" and this well of Nectar of Naam lies within us: "Antar koohnta Amrit bharia" p-570. Religious and spiritual education has been taken out of public school curriculum under secular governments. The new generation is totally devoid of spiritual education from home or school. Spirituality is questioned by rationalists because they cannot see the spirit, mind or God. So soul is being called DNA; mind, the 'Jot Saroop', is being called the brain. The brain is just a processer of communication from the five sensory organs of our body to the mind, and the orders of our mind then communicate to the five work organs of the body to do karmas.

Everything spiritual- its existence is denied for it is not visible to our eyes or other senses. Same is true for God. But the scientific, logical and rationalists wont like to be called atheists and still talk of God as not responsible for creation but believe in the theory of existentialism, the Big Bang Theory of Creation, and the Theory of Evolution of Species by Darwin. The Soul is considered as DNA and is destroyed at death and hence, there will be no reincarnation. So many basic doctrines of Sikhi, as given in Gurbani, are considered a philosophy which should be replaced with new scientific findings. Now scientists appear to have found physical parallels for spiritual entities via energy for God, DNA for Soul, brain for mind etc. Most of the people are gullible to the above scientific replacements as they can visualize it intellectually. So our mind without Naam, as per Gurbani, is like a lost fool: "Bin Naavay jug kamla phiray" p-643. Not knowing who we really are, our mind is being run by five doots (kaam, krodh, lobh, moh and hankar) of Maya. In this age, of Kaljug Guru Ji rightly calls us demons or 'pret'. But in Satjug we were Gurmukhs (swan):

"Kal meh pret jini Ram na pshata.
Satjug param huns beechaari." p-1131

Discussions can go on, but none can be intellectually convinced about the spiritual truths in Gurbani unless they accept the fundamental reality of the existence of God, the Immortal Creator Being who is manifesting within all live beings as the soul. All our consciousness, wisdom and intelligence come from God: "Surat matt chaturaee Teri Tu jnaa-ay jaana Ram" p-779. Within a fool and wise man is the same soul (He makes the two minds different) but the biggest fool is one who does not accept Naam (Soul/ God):

"Moorakh siaana ek hain ek Jot do-ay naaon.
Moorakhaan sir moorakh hai jo mannay naheen Naaon." p-1015

It takes years of research in a science lab to come up with new findings and a few more years before it can really be marketed for profits and gains for the research. It seems for religion and spirituality; we want to first see the results before we invest any time in it. God is kind enough to take care of the ungrateful, too, as they are also His children. Nanak says He is always so forgiving:

"Akirtghna noon palda Nanak sud bakhsind." p-293

Should such gurmat discussions like 'no soul', and hence 'no God', no reincarnation, no Naam japna go on forever? This is confusing the gullible Sikhs who are trying to learn about Gurmat in this group. Does the forum have any policy or framework which defines Gurmat, which guides the members to limit their discussions within that framework so as not to propagate any anti-gurmat ideas?

UNDERSTANDING GURBANI: PART-1

Gurbani is the utterance of Gurus and Bhagats who had all realized God and had become one with Him. They were all in their sehaj state/ chautha pud/ turiya awastha where their thinking is not controlled by the three gunas of maya of the material world. Their budhi is not intellectual like ours, which is based on knowledge of the physical world but bibek which is gained from the Satguru who gives spiritual knowledge about God and His creation:

"Bibek budh Satgur te paaee gur giaan guru Har kera." p-711

So Gurmat, or teachings of Gurbani, is true knowledge about the True God, His creation, and our role and responsibilities in it. So, Gurus and Bhagats have used the best means to express this spiritual information using exquisite poetry of all forms; meters set to raagaas and taals in which the message came and they sang in it. To the Pothi, Guru Gobind Singh added Gurbani of Guru Tegh Bahadur Ji and this was later given the Guruship by Guru Gobind Singh Ji in 1708 at Nander Sahib. Guru Gobind Singh Ji then called it the Guru Granth Sahib. The Guru Granth Sahib is a Scripture par excellence for the age of Kaljug showing us the right way of living and emancipation.

Although, it is written in Gurmukhi script- it contains many dialects of Punjabi, Sant Bhasha and other languages from where Bhagats lived. It also contains hymns written in Sanskrit and Persian. The knowledge provided in it has references to various ancient scriptures like Vedas, Puranas, Simraties and Kuran. To understand it, one needs to be not only a scholar of languages but also well versed in Indian scriptures and philosophies and truths given, therein.

It is a scripture for a serious spiritual seeker who desirers seeking union with God, the Creator of this entire universe, and is running it in under His Will and Hukam. It shows the path to our real self as mind/soul the child of God and ultimate source of life. God is realized through deep mediation on Him and raising our consciousness above the physical level to a sunn or thoughtless state of mind in which the entire spiritual world where God lives.

Most of the Gurbani deals with the passage from this physical world to spiritual world and the final emancipation from it to reach our true home. We came to do our karmas in this world as per God's plan. There are words used for the other world and unseen world like sunn, chautha pud and dasam duaar. Nij Ghar, Sach Ghar, turiya awastha, lok parlok, dharam raj, chittar gupt, jumdoot, aava gavan, panj doots, raj gun, sat gun, tum gun of Maya and Kaal and many more relating to the invisible spiritual world are there but not believable to a manmukh.

This knowledge is written in poetry and not in prose, using a grammar different from modern Punjabi making it difficult to interpret unless one is familiar with the subject matter. The knowledge is separated not by chapters on different subjects but by raagaas. To understand each hymn, one needs not only a dictionary for the language but also an overall knowledge of the entries in Gurmat Gian. Till one has experienced the different spiritual states, one is not able to comprehend Gurbani and will read it with totally wrong meanings derived from his intellectual wisdom rather than spiritual wisdom which comes from Guru within us.

To understand Gurbani correctly, one needs the blessings of the Guru and the sangat of a true sant, saadh or bhagat who has experienced it all by himself and understands the spiritual stages Gurbani is showing. Gurbani is not just for reading or paying our obeisance but to be studied, understood and acted upon the message it gives to really gain from it. It is the duty of every Sikh to read it and accept everything Guru Ji is saying as Truth:

"Gursikh meet chalo Gur chaalee.
Jo Gur kahay soee bhall manion Har Har Har kathaa niraalee." p-667

UNDERSTANDING GURBANI: PART-2

Gurbani, as discussed earlier, is our Guru and source of spiritual knowledge to guide us here on this planet where we, the spiritual beings, are on a physical journey. Living on this planet, we are all absorbed or lost into Maya and its three Gunas dealing with only the physical side. We then are disconnected from our spiritual source- the Jot that our mind is. There are obstacles we face in understanding Gurbani which were discussed previously and will be listed briefly here before the discussion.

1. Although, the language of our Gurus is Punjabi, it is an older version of Punjabi and some words are hard to understand without the help of a good dictionary.

2. Gurbani is written in poetry and it is not easy to make out meanings of the sentences unless one is already familiar with the subject matter and the poetic order, as it does not follow the rules of prose.

3. There is a serious problem in how to express the spiritual phenomena in the language for which it does not have words for that realm. This is because our language relates only to physically observable and measurable things, as recognized by our five senses. However, spiritual phenomena lies above the cognizance of the five senses, and hence our intelligence which is trained to deal with the physical realm only and cannot comprehend it and often doesn't believe in it or rejects it. So this is a hurdle in expressing spirituality in our language and understanding it when expressed using similes, metaphors and allegories. So, the

meanings could be translated at a physical plane or rejected as a mythology.

4. The spiritual teachings are not presented, like in a textbook for our temporal knowledge, where every idea is taken up separately and we are led further into that realm, step by step. In Sri Guru Granth Sahib, spiritual wisdom is spread all over and one has to dig out the knowledge by searching it as if looking for pearls in a deep sea.

5. One needs to be really dedicated to searching the spiritual truths and devoted to the Path of Truth and truthful living. When one is imbued with Naam/Sabad, understanding of Gurbani comes through the help of Guru himself: "Gur kee Banee Gur te jatee je Sabad ratte rang laa-ay" p-1346. Here Guru is Sabad Guru as explained below.

6. One needs to seek the company of people who have travelled on this path of spirituality, as entailed in Gurbani, and having reached the Param Pud or Chautha Pud. They know the path, which Guru Ji is telling in Gurbani and can advise the novice correctly. Guru Ji calls them Sant, Sadh, Bhagat and Brahmgiani and guide us to find their Sangat which Guru Ji calls sadhsangat and satsangat. It is not easy to find their company but for those who are true seekers, God Himself connects them with the true guides. Seek and thou shall find:

"Hum Santan sio bun aaee.
Poorab likhiaa paaee." p-1374

7. There are languages other than Punjabi in Gurbani, with which one is not familiar with. However one does not have to know and understand every hymn and line of Sri Guru Granth Sahib to understand all the truths. The spiritual secrets and truths are presented repeatedly in every raag and in many a shabad in every raag. Sometimes, Guru Ji gives a complete map of a spiritual journey briefly in one shabad or pauri.

8. Translations are a good source of help in understanding the meanings of difficult words; but translations of the whole line, or

shabad, may not be accurate as it depends upon the spiritual state of the translator and whether he is a seeker or just an academic translator. The truest translation will be done by a true Sant or the one who is in Chautha Pad, but we don't have one such available and have to look for such a Saint. Till then, try on your own through Naam Japna to meet with the Guru (Sabad) within you who will help you on this path:

"Giaan anjan Gur deeaa.
Agiaan andher binaas." p-293

Here are some of the common misunderstandings of the basics of Gurmat caused by the factors mentioned above:

1. Name, Naam and Naam Japna

The word Naam written in Punjabi reads the same as the word which means Name, whereas Naam has an absolutely different meaning in Gurbani. Name in Gurbani means Name of God and there are so many names given in Gurbani for God like Ram, Hari, Gopal, Narayan, Keshav, Beethlaa and so on. Naam in Gurbani means Divine Power/Hukam/Sabad/Jyot/Spiritual Wealth/Spiritual Intelligence/ Consciousness and so on. Sat Naam is mostly interpreted as Name of God is Truth whereas it means God's Naam is True (like God as it is extension of God Himself in His creation): "Aapinay aap saajio aapeenay rachio naaon" p-463. Naam as Sabad is called Sabad Guru and: "Sabad Guru Surat dhun chela" p-943. Naam is same as God:

"Gur Gobind Gobind Guru hai Nanak bhed na bhaee." p-422

Where the word 'naam' is linked to the act of utterance it means name, otherwise it is Naam: 'Naaon (Naam) Tera Nirankaar hai naa-ay (name) laeeay (jappeeay to link with Naam) narak na jaee-ay." Naam (name) jappo ji aisay aisay.", "Naa-ay (name) suniay naaon (Naam) upjay naamay (from Naam) vadiaaee" p-1240. By listening to His Name, that produces Naam in mind and this Naam brings honor," Laaj muray jo naon (name) na laivay. Naam (Naam) bihona sukhi kion hovay " p-1148. Those who do not remember His name should die in shame. Without His Naam, nobody can be happy. So we have to distinguish between name and Naam to interpret Gurbani correctly.

Naam japna is simply focusing the attention of the mind on the sound/ dhun of recitation of name of God called 'gurmantra' (Waheguru for Sikhs) in a rhythmic manner doing it with devotion. After sometime, the consciousness goes inside the body and it is called sunn/samadhi state. In this state, the mind stops thinking and is not aware of the body. Naam is inside the body: "Nau nidh Amrit Prabh ka Naam. Dehi meh is ka bisraam" p-293 and our mind has surti, or consciousness, and has a chance to meet it there. This state may last only for few minutes in the beginning. When a thought appears in the mind, surti comes out and one is awake. After regular practice one will first start hearing Anhad Sabad in the ears while awake and later may be lucky to hear in sunn. That is mind connecting with Sabad, or Naam, and it starts cleansing the mind: "Oh dhopay naavay kay rung" p-4. Regular practice in Japana will lead to hearing Sehaj Dhun and then Toor and Naad, which precedes the Vision of Naam as very bright Light which removes all the doubts and duality: "Naam Japat kot soor ujiarra binse bharam andhera" p-700. This makes the mind pure and then one has to wait for the Gurparsad or Grace of God to bring the mind into the Sehaj State and unite it with the Supreme Being. The union is preceded by Panch Sabad or the five melodies of Sabad and leads to permanent bliss/anand when all the five doots of Maya fall under the control of the mind and the troubles of Kaal vanish:

"Vaajay Panch Sabad titt Ghar subhaage.
Ghar subhaage Sabad vaajay kalaa jitt kar dhaariaa.
Panch doot tudh vuss keetay Kaal kantak maaria." p-971

Different stages of spiritual evolution are discussed in Gurbani again and again, reminding us not to miss the goal of human life to unite with our Source, God, to achieve permanent happiness and bliss.

Naam Japna only serves to bring the mind into sunn and the rest is done by Sabad Guru who sits inside each one of us and it is Sabad Guru which connects us with Naam and prepares us for the union. Guru Ji calls Sabad Guru as Satguru, also: "Satgur meraa sadaa sadaa naa aavay naa jaavay. Oh abinaasee Purakh hai jo sabh meh rahiaa smaa-ay" p-759. The immortal Satgur lives inside everybody: "Satgur vich aap rakhion kar pargat aakh sunaaia" p-466. God, Himself, places the Satgur within everybody. When the disciple is ready Satguru speaks to him through Sabad.

To prepare for Naam Japna, one has to acquire other good qualities also by being truthful in thought, words and deeds: "Vin gun keetay bhagat na hoay" p-4. Also, one has to live a temporal life and serve others, and seek the company of saintly people.

UNDERSTANDING GURBANI: PART-3

This subject was discussed twice before in Part-1 and Part-2 where I discussed the Name, Naam and Naaon. In this missive, I will briefly discuss how to bring out the difference between Gurbani and Sabad. Word Sabad appears in Gurbani as Sabad- Guru also and is mostly mistaken for written Gurbani whereas Sabad is utterance of the Divine. This misunderstanding throws us off the direction of the spiritual path to God where Sabad alone helps and guides us to meet with our Divine Source from where Sabad is coming from.

SABAD AND GURBANI

Sabad in Gurbani means Divine utterance like Anhad Sabad, Sehaj Dhun, Anhad Bani, Taar Ghor Bjantar, Naad, Toor and Panch Sabad. Gurbani is the utterance of Gurus and Bhagats, which is written in the Guru Granth Sahib in human language which explains about God, His Sabad, His creation, His presence in His creation and how He is running the whole universe under His Hukam/Control. Gurbani also explains to us how we turn away from God by temptation or the lure of Maya- which acts in the Three Gunas and captivates our mind. Gurbani also tells how to achieve freedom from this hold of Maya with the help of Naam Japna. This connects us with the Utterance of God, or Sabad, inside each one of us which leads to Naam and finally illumines our mind with His Jot and purifies it to a state where we have a chance to go back to our original spiritual Home, Nij Ghar with Gurparsad, the Grace of God. Following Gurbani quotes will explains the above statements. God created the entire universe with His one utterance:

"Keeta pasaao eko kwaao." p-3

This was done by His Sabad and He destroys His creation by His Sabad and then recreates it by His Sabad:

"Uttpat parlo Sabday hovay.
Sabday he phir opat hovay." p-117

Guru Ji states that He speaks through each one of His creation by His Sabad:

"Sabhay ghat Ram bolay." p-988

His Sabads in Gurbani are mentioned as Anhad Sabad, Panch Sabad, Naad, Anhad Toor, Sehaj Dhun and Taar Ghor Bajantar:

"Ghat ghat vaajay Naad." p-6
"Sub meh Sabad vartay Prabh Sachaa." p-1275
"Binwant Nanak gur charan laagay vaajay anhad tooray." p-922
"Anhad baani naad vajaaia." p-375
"Vaajay panch sabad tit ghar subhagay." p-917
"Taar ghor bajantar teh Sach takhat sultan." p-1291

Guru Ji further states that life force in the living beings is because of this Sabad and it is through this Sabad that one meets with the Husband Lord:

"Jeean anadar Jeeo Sabad hai jit Sauh milaava hoay." p-1250

Thus, this Sabad is the Soul or God (Life force, intelligence, our human nature and consciousness) in each one of us. Guru Ji also states that Naam is evolved from Sabad and it is through this Sabad that we meet with Creator God:

"Sabday hee Naaon upjay Sabday mail milaaia." p-644

So- Sabad, Naam and Soul are the same part of God in His creations which connects or links our mind with Him or His Consciousness. Guru Ji also states that it is from this Sabad that this holy Baani evolved and the Gurmukhs (Gurus and Bhagats) uttered it for us to hear:

"Sabday upjay Amrit Baani Gurmukh aakh sunaavania." p-125

The Sabad which sounds in living beings and the entire universe has been called Anahad Sabad, the unending and unstruck divine melody or Word of God. The Creator God has staged His wondrous play. He makes us hear His divine music of Sabad:

"Tin Kartay ik chalat upaaia.
Anhad Banee Sabad sunaaia." p-117

God's Sabad sounds in so many different ways and through His Sabad He resides everywhere in His universe:

"Sabad ghaneray Har Prabh Teray.
Tu karta sabh thaneen." p-775

Can we hear His Sabad or Anhad Bani? Yes, we can but normally we don't. A mind under the influence of Maya is spiritually deaf and blind, and cannot hear it. Instead what it hears is meaningless uproar and tumult:

"Maya dharee utt unnah bola.
Sabad na sunay bauh rol ghacholaa." p-313

Those who cannot hear the Sabad are munmukh:

"Se manmhkh jo Sabad naa pachhaanay." p-1054

Without the Sabad, they are blind and deaf and their whole life in this world is wasted:

"Sabad na jaanay se unnhay bolay se kit aa-ay sansaaraa." p-601

To hear the Sabad, the mind has to stop the noise of thoughts of the three gunas (Maya). For this, the mind has to stop wandering outside and escaping through the nine doors of the body, come in and reach the tenth door and into its own spiritual home, 'nij ghar'. There the divine melody of the Sabad resounds day and night. Only following Guru's teachings can this be done:

"Nau darvaajay dhavat rahay dasvay nij ghar vaasaa paa-ay. Othay Sabad vajay din raatee gurmattee Sabad sunavanian." p-954

The tenth door is not easy to open. It can be done only with the help of Gursabad which is Gurmantar:

"Bajar kpaat naa khulanee Gursabad khulijay." p-954

These Sabads are heard when the consciousness goes inside the sunn state during Naam Japna and the devotee's mind is cleansed enough by Naam. When heard in sunn, the devotee is supposed to focus attention on it. Guru Nanak Ji calls it Sabad Guru and our surti inside its chelaa:

"Sabad Guru surat dhun chela." p-943

In Gurbani, Sabad Guru is also called Satguru or Guru, Naam and Amritsar as this washes the 'koor thee paal', which is the wall of falsehood of maya over the mind, making it pure to receive Pure Naam and ultimate union with the Pure One:

"Mun maila Sach nirmalaa kio kar miliaa jaa-ay.
Prabh mailay ta mil rahay haumay sabad jalaa-ay." p-480

In understanding the Sabad, as discussed above, it is very obvious that:

1. Gurbani is the utterance of Gurus and Bhagats and written down in SGGS.
2. Sabad is theutterance of God, is unending and non-struck divine melody which not only created physical universe but also goes on in it and all creations of God.
3. God's presence in our bodies is with this Sabad which is called Soul, Naam and Jot.
4. Gurbani is evolved from this Sabad of God. Gurus and Bhagats uttered it and wrote it.
5. The only way to reach God for a human mind is to connect with Sabad which cleanses our mind and leads us to Naam. After the cleansing of the mind- it finally connects it to God with His Grace.
6. Gurbani Guru is showing us the way to connect with Sabad Guru, who is an extension of God, Himself, in us through Naam Japna.
7. The ultimate Guru/Satguru is God, Himself, who created Sabad/ Naam and sent Guru Ji in human form to show us the way and wrote down the instructions in human languages. This collection of Gurbani in SGGS is The True Guru for us to read, understand and follow.

WHY SO MANY INTERPRETATION OF GURBANI

Gurbani is not a text book on religion, written chapter-wise on different aspects of religion. It deals with spirituality, the reality of the unseen that we are; mind, soul and God and their play in the material world called His universe- physically visible and invisible. This play carries responsibility for good and bad results, not knowing that they were doing all this because of somebody else's control. And when they realize what reality is, they write:

"Mera mujh mehn kush nahin jo kissh hai so tera." p-1375

God creates different creatures out of Himself and separates them from Himself thus making them think they are on their own and makes them play the roles He wants them to play. They go through happiness and grief, not knowing why but He uses them to perform different roles in His divine play which has been going on for an unknown amount of time. But we think it started with our life only and because of good and bad karma. We think the world is running to some definite set of rules which don't change, whereas He is changing His game plan as He likes. Sometimes He creates new worlds and destroys it like we destroy sand castles on the beach.

To some, He makes them realize the Truth of His game and takes them back to Himself, whereas all others are still lost in the moh (attachment) of Maya and are playing in His drama. They do this without knowing about this game and suffer and cry, yet can't do anything unless they listen and understand what His messengers like Guru Ji are telling us as to how to get out of the vicious cycles of life, death and miseries involved in life. All our intelligence and wisdom is given to us by Him whereas, we think it is our own, "Sikh matt sabh budh tumari" and we call others ignorant or wise. So according to our own understanding we try to interpret Gurbani:

"Aap aapni budh hai jeti.
Barnat bhin bhin tohe teti." -Benate Chaupaee

Guru Ji calls this play of God 'akath katha', which means the indescribable story in which the mind, which is the child of God, is separated from Him and goes through all the different roles He made for him and finally He makes him come home and unite with Him by connecting the mind with His 'sabad', His utterance, which goes on in the entire universe. But we, separated from Him, don't hear it because our senses are dulled with thoughts of Maya:

"Maya dhaaree utt unnaah bola sabad naa sunhi bauh rol ghchola."
p-313

To some, He connects with Gurbani, Sadhsangat and makes them do Japna on His Name, making them hear His sabad to connect them with Him. He makes them realize their true self and that they are part of His Jot, or Light, and they become one with Him. In that, they understand His entire Play of Life that is going on.

It is about this play that Guru Ji and other Bhagats wrote about in Gurbani in the Sri Guru Granth Sahib, after they understood this game. What they wrote was experienced by them in the fourth stage (chautha pud) of spiritual elevation and they perceived it but did not intellectually visualize it. They had to bring the spiritual story down to our own language, which is not fit for describing the indescribable. So, there is a barrier of easy description in our language of the material world. So they had to use similes and metaphors. Naam is called "Nau nidh "or a "jewel". Our soul, when it leaves the body, is called 'huns' or swan and the presence of Naam in our body is called Amritsar, or pool of nectar. The mind needs food, which is Naam, and we don't even understand it but Guru Ji advises us to earn food for the mind like we earn for feeding our body. This is done by Naam Japna but how many of us understand it:

"Har Har nit jappio ji laha khatio dehari." p-981

Our misunderstanding carries on. Our ignorance of the spiritual world and its description in Gurbani is totally misconstrued in physical connotations, missing the true meaning of Gurbani.

This knowledge is given to the minds who have realized Him. Guru Ji calls them 'sants' and tells them they should go tell this indescribable story to others as to how to meet God, "Kahe Nanak suno santo kathio akath kahaani" p-918. No wonder Guru Ji keeps telling us to find a true saint and seek the dust of his feet, which really means that we should seek the knowledge of traveling on the path to The True One. Do we really seek such a person? No. We think we can understand everything reading Gurbani. And also reading Gurbani is everything.

This is the state of the translators who could be good scholars in language and scriptures but devoid of spiritual experiences which shows the true meaning as described in Gurbani. So, they interpret Gurbani according to their intellectual and spiritual level, and since everyone is different from each other they have different understandings.

For the most accurate translation of Gurbani, we need somebody who has traveled the path of spirituality and has experienced it, seen and realized God. It is difficult but we got to find such a person. He may not be a scholar or a scientist because the literate or illiterate can achieve spiritual knowledge:

"Parhia unparhia Param Gut paavay." p-148.

TO DEATH AND AFTER: PART-1

Birth and death relate to the physical body we are born into by His Will. We are all spiritual beings, children of God, and are here as per His plan to take part in a God created play in which we are mere actors to play certain roles which He assigns to us according to what He thinks fit for us in this life time. He arranged this play according to His own plan and enjoys watching it:

"Apna khel Aap kar dekhay Thakur rachan rachaaya." p-272

All species on this planet, the complete solar system and beyond is involved in our life as we are all affected by all that is happening around us. We affect our own environment too, which reacts to changes we bring in it; whether physical, social and spiritual. The complete system is God's creation and running under His Hukam, or Will, to a certain order which He set. But He controls it as to whatever He wants to do with it:

"Hukmay andar sabh ko bahar Hukam naa koay." p-1

The physical universe is made out of five components; air (gaseous), water (liquid), fire (energy), earth (material) and sky (space). These five components and the universe were created by Naam, God's extension into His physical universe which Naam created:

"Naamay hee tay sabh kich hoaa" p-753
"Naam kay dharay khand brahmand." p-284

"Naam kay dharay sagal akaar." p-284
"Apeenay aap saajio Apeenay rachio Naaon.
Dooee kudrat sajeeay kar asan ditho chaao." p-453

God sits within each of His creations as Naam, and His presence in us is called Soul. Naam, or Soul, is immortal like Him and is the source of life and consciousness in us. God also provides intellect, wisdom and instructions to us. The mind which is given the above tools to use to plan and execute deeds or karmas we are supposed to do here during our life on this planet:

"Sikh matt sabh budh tumaari." p-753

Our mind, along with its consciousness, wisdom and intelligence is constructed in Saram Khand:

"Tithay ghariay surat matt mun budh." p-8

Mind, which is the physical embodiment of Light/Jot of God/Soul, has the duty is to realize itself while in the human body:

"Mun too jot saroop hain apna mool pchhan." p-441

Mind is made up of five subtle components of creation and is here to do its karma and dutiful deeds:

"Eh mun karma eh mun dharma eh mun panch tutt tay janmaa."
p-415

Mind stays in this body; is fixed by time and the number of breaths; the body is allowed and cannot be changed:

"Gin ghalay sabh divas sass.
Naa badhan ghatan til saar." p-254

Mind is pulled out of this body when the time of its stay is over. As it came under His Hukam, so it goes back as per His Hukam after doing the work it was supposed to do:

"Jaisa cheery likhiaa tehay karam kmaa-ay.
Ghalay aa-vay Nanakaa saday uthay jaa-ay." p-1239

Mind is an extension of Soul to deal with physical world and is immortal like soul, which is placed in the mother's womb the same time as it gets pregnant, where the body is built for it:

"Saahay kay pharmaray ji dehi vich jeeo aa-ay paiaa." p-1007

Mind and soul are enclosed in a subtle body tied inside the physical body, which is delivered into this world when it is ready. Life for the mind begins on this planet with the first breath the body takes. The subtle body is tied inside the physical body at a point below the belly button called 'dharan or mool duaar':

"Mool duaaray bandhiaa bandh." p-1159

Besides the Soul/Naam and mind inside the body, there are other spiritual beings in the body installed as per God's plan. Each of them has a job to do with mind's stay in the body. They are:

1. Dharam Raj, the judge of mind's thoughts and deeds while in body:

"Nanak jee upaaykay likh naavayn Dharam bhaalia. p-463

He is under strict orders of God to judge truthfully and has the angel/demon of death under his command:

"Dharam Rai noo Hukam hai beh sacha dhram beechar. Doojay bha-ay dusht atma oh teri sarkaa. p-38

2. Chittar Gupt, the auditor and reporter who has strict records of each of mind's actions and thoughts in each breath the body takes. There are three areas in which mind thinks or acts in the world of Maya and they are:

    a. Tum Gun: which deals with five doots of Maya; lust, anger, greed, attachment and ego.
    b. Raj Gun: which deals with ambitions, worries, anxieties while interacting with people and earning its living.
    c. Sat Gun: relates to actions for spiritual growth like being humble, compassionate, helpful, serving others, praying to and remembrance of God:

"Raj gun, tum gun sat gun kheeay eh teree sab Mayaa." p-1123

The full account of the mind's life, in number of breaths spent at each Gun, is submitted to Dharam Raj after the last breath or death of the physical body.

3. Jumdoot, whose job is to open the knot where subtle body is tied inside the physical body, pulls the subtle body with the mind out after the body has taken the last breath as per His Will. This is done under strict order form God:

"Khulee ganth uto likhiaa aaia Ram." p-111

The five doots of Maya: lust, anger, greed, attachment and ego who are the servants of the mind and are necessary for its life in 'bhavjal sagr' in the physical body. But, they take over the mind for its lure of these desires and it becomes their slave. The life of the mind under the control of the five doots of Maya makes it ignorant of its spiritual source and turns it into munmukh. Then, it has to learn its reality under the guidance of Satguru and Gurmukhs to be freed from these five, which makes it Gurmukh and it unites with God and ends the cycle of births and deaths in this world. This is the prime goal of human life and this can happen only in human form:

"Bhaee prapat manukh dehureea.
Gobind milan kee eho teree baria." p-12

Kaal is in charge of the world of Maya and runs the universe for God under His order. God has handed over the entire operation of the universe to it:

"Khand ptaal deep sabh loaa Kaalay vus aap Prabh keea." p-1076

Kaal represents time and death, which is in Gurbani and governs the three gunnas of Maya:

"Traiy gun Kaalay kee sirkara." p-231

The Physical death is the departure of the subtle body, also called 'huns' (the swan soul), from the physical body for good. What happens to the mind after death will be discussed in part-2.

TO DEATH AND AFTER: PART-2

Our life in the body is governed by Prana, or breaths, allocated to us for our lifetime. Our real wealth is the breaths given to us by the Almighty and it is called 'dhan' (wealth) in Gurbani. As we utilize our last breath, our life is over in the body and our real self, who is contained in the subtle or sookham body; invisible to our eyes, is pulled out by Jum- the scary angel of death. And we have to give an account of what we thought and did in our lifetime. We are summoned to report immediately to the court of Dharam Raj. The order comes from God and is passed on to us:

"Amal sirano lekha deena. Aa-ay kathan doot jum lena.
Kiaa tai khattiaa kiaa gvaaia. Chalau sitaab Dewaan bulaaia.
Chal darhaal Dewaan bulaaia. Har phurmaan dargah kaa aaiaa."
p-792

As the jum shows the mind the order of God and opens the knot where the sookham body is tied to the physical body, it requests the mind to leave the body as per the order of God:

"Khuli ganth utho likhiaa aaia Ram." p-1110

If the person is a Gurmukh, he is already aware of his time of departure from the body, listens to the loud sound of 'toor'- a signal for exit from the body. The Gurmukh immediately pulls his 'surt' in, focusing on the trai-kuti and moves to where the sound is coming from, the divine home; the Nij Ghar. He is already familiar with the route, as he has won a place in his spiritual home- having been blessed to be a 'jiwanmukt' because of his devotional worship and imbued with Naam:

"Gurmukh aavay jaa-ay nisang." p-932

Jum is not allowed to hear the Sabad and runs away so that Lord does not punish him:

"Sabad sunay taan doorauh bhaa-gay.
Mat maaray Har jeeo veparvaha hay." p-1054

Gurmukh enters the Nijmehal and meets the Lord amidst the sounding of anhad Sabads. Among all the live beings and physical creatures of God's kingdom, the Gurmukh wins honor from Him:

"Gurmukh jaa-ay milay nijmehli anhad Sabad bjaavaigo.
Jee jant sabh sist upaaee Gumukh sobha paavaigo." p-1310

Gurmukh is blessed by God, Naam abides in his heart and he hears the unstruck melody of Divine music. He is at peace and respected by all as a saintly person. Jum dares not even come near him:

"Jisay nivaajay Gurmukh saajay Naam vassay tis anhad vaajay.
Tis he sukh tis he thakuraaee tisay naa aa-vay jum nera." p-1082.

However, a munmukh whose mind is asleep under influence of Maya: "Mun soiaa maya bismaad", do not understand the message of jum. So, jum hits him on the head. He wakes up and repents (over what he did in life) but cannot escape by running away:

"Jum ko dund pario sir ooper tab sovat teh jaagio.
Khaa hoat ab kiaa pashtaa-ay choottat nahin bhagio." p-1008

Manmukh had never heard this loud Sabad before; he gets scared and runs to the jum for help. Jum arrests him to bring him to Dharam Raj, humiliating him on the way under order:

"Dootan non phurmaaia lai chalay pat gvaa-ay." p-417

As the soul and mind in sookham leaves the body, the body starts disintegrating into its basic components; earth, fire, water and becomes a poisonous river of fire. The mind faces this and has to cross this fiery river of poisonous flames. There is none else there. The ocean of fire spits out waves of searing flames, the self willed manmukh falls into it and is roasted over there:

"Aagay Bimal nadi agan bikh jhela.
Tithay avar naa koee jeeo akelaa.
Bhar bhar agan saagar de kehri parh dujhay manmukh taee hay."
p-1026

It is like an unfathomable ocean of fire, only the roar of pitiful cries can be heard. O Nanak, there it does not matter whether you were a king or an emperor:

"Jithay saair langhna agan panee asgah.
Kandhi dis naa aavaee dhaee pavay khah.
Nanak othay janeeay sah koee paatsah." p-12

Terrible Jumdoot tries to crush you like seeds in an oil press, only the Name of God can be of help there:

"Jah mahan bhaiaan doot jum dalaiy.
Teh kewal Naam sung teraiy chalaiy." p-264

Mind, afraid of going through these fires, begs the jumdoot to save him as he did lot of good deeds and charities. But jumdoot cannot help him and tells him that for good deeds and charities, one still has to go to Dharam Raj:

"Pun daan jo beejday Dharam Rai kai jaaee." p-1414

He is advised that the wealth he valued is all left behind. He should have earned the wealth of Naam, in having which- he did not have to get beaten up on his head:

"So dhan mitt na kadheeay jit sir chottan khaa-ay." p-1287

The money he earned during his whole life and carried the burden of like a coolly; he only got a little bit of it for daily use. Rest is all left behind for others:

"Bharree kau ohau bharra miliaa hore sagal bhaiaa bigaana." p-497

Self-willed munmukh who was neither aware of nor cared to earn the wealth of Naam wasted all the wealth of the breaths of life; the capital given to him. The munmukh, having lost his capital, is punished in the Court of the Lord:

"Munmukh mool gwaaia dargah miliay sajaay." p-1331

In the Court of the Dharam Raj, the munmukh's account is examined and the sinners are crushed like the seeds in a press:

"Dar la-ay lekha peer chhuttay Nanaka jion tail." p-473

When the manmukh is questioned for his actions, he is severely beaten. Nobody can help him there and no one listen to his cries:

"Manmhukh agaiy laikha mangeeay bauhti hovay maar.
Othey hath na appray kook na sunay pookaar." p-1280

Manmukh cries now for help and calls his family as nobody is coming to help him. Kabir Ji comments on his situation that he has overlooked the worship and meditation on God's Name. The manmukh was so busy in raising family. He was busy running his business and now neither the brothers nor the relatives come to help him:

"Kabir Har ka simran shaad kay paalio bauhat kutumbh.
Dhandaah kartaa rah gaiaa bhaee rahiaa naa bandh." p-1370

Finally, his account is presented to Dharam Raj and his account is settled. What happens next will be discussed in Part-3.

TO DEATH AND AFTER: PART-3

At the end of the lifetime given to the body by the Almighty, the body dies and the mind, the ruler of the body, "Kaayan nagri eh mun raja," leaves the body and is escorted out of it by the order of the Almighty. According to its spiritual state- if the mind is Gurmukh, Sabad leads it to Nij Ghar; and if the mind is manmukh to jumdoot, the scary angel of death arrests it and leads it to Dharam Raj, the Spiritual Judge where an account of its deeds is presented. He reviews the report prepared by Chaittar Gupt, presents it to God Himself who makes the final judgment and write the destiny of the mind for the next life and none are exempt from it:

"Sabhna jeean sir lekh Dhurahoon bin lekhaiy naheen koee jeeo."
p-598

Bags full of reports of the mind are presented in the Court of the Lord where the true deeds (done under Naam) and the false deeds (done under Maya) are sorted out:

"Nanak badra maal ka bheetar dhariaa aan.
Khotay kharay parkheean Sahib kay deeban." p-789

Dharam Raj is told to check where the mind has spent all the breaths given. He reads out that this mind was born in pain, died in pain and dealt with pain while living in the physical world. The more he reads, the more the pains show; his whole life was heaps of pain and no peace is seen here:

"Dukh vich jaman dukh maran dukh vartan sansaar.
Dukh dukh aggay aakheeay parh parh kareh pukaar.
Dukh keea pandaan khuleeaan sukh naa nikalio koay." p-1240

Dukh comes from spending the breaths in Maya or falsehood, and sukh comes in spending the breaths in Naam and in God's remembrance. In this case, the mind has spent all its life in falsehood and did not work in accordance with the Will of God. So for the case of a habitual sinner, he is to be sent where sinners belong. The home of the sinner is in fire. It keeps burning and cannot be extinguished. He does not go to see where the Lord is being worshipped. He abandons the Lord's Path and takes the wrong path. He forgets the Primal Lord God and is caught in the cycle of reincarnation:

"Papee kaa ghar agnay maahay. Jalat rhaiy mitway kab naahay. Har kee bhagat naa daikhay jaa-ay. Marag shod amarag paa-ay. Moolauh bhoolaa aa-vay jaa-ay." p-116

Such false persons are cast upside down in the womb and punished there repeatedly and go through cycles of reincarnation; without Naam they lose their honor:

"Khoto putho raaleeay bin Naavay pat jaa-ay." p-1330

The fickle minded person is struck down (by jum) so many times. Having lost this opportunity (of Holy company), he has no place for comfort. Cast into the womb for reincarnation, a self-willed munmukh lives as a worm in dung:

"Mun chanchal bauh chhottan khaa-ay.
Etho chhuttkia thaur naa paa-ay.
Garabh joan vistaan kaa vaas.
Titt ghar manmukh karay nivaas." p-362

Munmukh does not know that he is born on this planet of death. He wastes his precious life in duality. He does not know his own self and trapped by doubts, he cries out in pain:

"Maran lakhaa-ay mandal meh aa-ay.
Janam pdaarath dubidha khovay.
Aap naa cheenas bharam bharam rovay." p-685

Guru Ji's advice to such a person is; you virtuless, ignorant child-dwell upon God forever. Cherish in your heart the One who created you. Nanak says He alone shall go with you:

"Nirguniaar iaaniaa so Prabh sadaa smahl.
Jin keea tis cheet rakh Nanak nibhaee naal." p-266

Further advice to munmukhs from Guru Ji is, 'At the time of death, nothing shall go along with you except the earnings of your devotion to God. All other wealth one earns in this world is like ashes. So earn the wealth of God's Naam and that is the only right wealth for you':

"Saath na chhalay bin bhajan bikhiaa sagli chhar.
Har Har Naam kmaavna Nanak eh dhan saar." p-288

Guru Ji has thrown light on the spiritual side of our life, which is real and not transitory unlike our physical life on this planet. We are part of the family of other spiritual beings of God. All that Guru Ji describes in the life after death is as per God's plan. They are not borrowed philosophies or fables of mythologies to scare us, as some believe. They are as real as the physical world we see with our eyes and other senses. Since we have not yet opened our spiritual eyes and we cannot yet see the spiritual world- we won't believe in it even when we say we believe in Guru Ji and Gurbani. What it really tells is that we still don't really believe in our Guru Ji, yet.

The fires Guru Ji is talking about are fires of the subtle spiritual world and they affect and burn our mind. We often feel it in this world, too, when someone says very harsh words to us. We often say 'what he said to me set my mind on fire.' These are the fires we often feel when dealing with our family members and others, as well as the fire that turns us against them and lead us to fight. Gurbani calls it 'agan sagar': "Agan sagar boodhat sansara." Jums are as real as the cops who come to arrest us when we commit crimes and when they beat us in captivity. But we have so identified ourselves with the physical nature that we don't believe that we are spiritual beings living in the spiritual world of our Father and Mother Parmaatmaa/ Hari/Gobind/ Akal Purakh/Waheguru. Guru Ji is constantly reminding us to wake from this sleep of maya and realize our self : "Jaag re mun jaagan haaray", who we really are and stop suffering pain and grief in the physical life; but to avail ourselves of this opportunity is to realize our own self and, hence, our Creator God who has all bliss for us. But we have no time to listen to the advice of Guru Ji even when they sacrificed their lives passing on this message to us.

I wrote all this with the kirpa of Guru Ji and the guidance of Gurmukhs who are always there when you tread on this path and come to help you. My zillions of thanks to them and Guru Ji, who is the shining star in every Sikh's life whether he/she cares or not to look at it and receive the light from it.

TO DEATH AND AFTER: PART-4

In Part-3, two extreme cases were discussed- one of a Gurmukh living in satgun only, and the other of a manmukh who lives away from satgun and spends his time mostly in rajgun and tamgun. But, there are many people who live their lives in combination of the three; some more in satgun, and the others more in rajgun or tamgun. So, how do they get judged for their good or bad karmas? This is what will be considered in this brief discussion under the guidance of Gurbani.

First, let us talk about a Gursikh who does all what Guru Ji requires a Sikh to do: pure in thought, word and deeds and does Naam Japna, too. He has acquired lot of fine qualities and some wealth of Naam; he hears Sabad, too, but could not make it to be one with God or find a permanent place in Nij Ghar for lacking acceptance from Waheguru, yet; or the inability to overcome the ego completely. Cases close to union with God are treated with respect and are given the joon of devtas. This place is called Dev Sthaan or Dev Lok in Gurbani. Guru Ji tells that there, one hears the Bani of Anhad Sabad all the time:

"Dev sthanay kiaa nisaani.
Teh baajay Sabad Anahad Bani." p-974

Minds of devtas are still in the three gunas and did not achieve the bliss of union with God, but are exempt from reincarnation. They get tired of this life and pray to God for giving them another chance in the human body in which they can put in more bhagti to achieve moksh:

"Is dehi ko simray dev. So dehi bhaj Har kee sev." p-1159

The very purpose of getting a human body is to do bhagti of God and we are advised by Guru Ji not to forget this prime purpose as a human:

"Bhajo Gobinid bhool matt jaao. Manas janam ka ehi laaho." p-1159

By God's blessings, they get another chance as a human and when awakened by this saintly company- they have no other interest in life but to make this their goal. Munmukhs do not understand them and call them lost or crazy. Yes, they are crazy to meet the Creator. They laugh, cry or keep quiet while lost in thoughts of their beloved Lord and care not about anybody else but The True One:

"Rung hassay rung rovay chup bhi kar jaa-ay.
Parvaah naaheen kisay keri baajh Sachay Naa-ay." p-473

Second, let us consider the case of a good human involved in the society but does spare time to ponder upon God and do Naam Japna. He is a fair balance of rajgun, tamgun and satgun and has acquired a small amount of wealth of Naam. Such persons are not judged harshly as they have some wealth of Naam and are given the next life as a human to continue further progress:

"Poorab janam parchoon kmaa-ay Har Har Har Naam piaray." p-982

How does one know one has a wealth of Naam? For seeking the spiritual wealth one has to connect with Naam, which lies inside our body, the source is Satguru- the Soul: "Nau nidh Amrit Parbh ka Naam. Dehi meh iskaa bisraam." This happens during Naam Japna when one is so absorbed into the dhun of jaap, one becomes thoughtless, the surti goes inside and connects with Naam- gaining wealth of Naam equivalent to the number of breaths spent in that mode.

God is kind and considerate enough to reward the person based on the strong desires the person had in his life. This happens to come out at the time of death. In the last breath, one sighs for what was most dear to the person. God tries to fulfill the desire of His child by giving him an opportunity in the next life. This is amply illustrated in the Shabad by Bhagat Tarlochan Ji at page 526. Two examples are given below:

If on the last breath one thinks of children, one is born as a female pig (who has many an offspring):

"Ant kaal jo bachay simray aisee chintaa meh jo maray.
Sookar joon val val autary." p-536

If on the last breath, one thinks of the house- one is born as a ghost (who is allowed to keep living in the same house):

"Ant kaal jo mandir simray aisaee chintaa meh jo maray.
Pret joon val val autary." p-526

If the last desire does not find expression in cases of death by accidents or in coma, judgment is based on the areas where most of the breaths were spent.

If majority of breaths were spent in tumgun, one is given birth in sea life.
If majority of breaths were spent in rujgun, one is given birth as birds of air.
If majority of breaths were spent in satgun, good deeds but no wealth of Naam, one is given birth on land as animal or vegetation.

Lots of animals or birds, which are pets of humans or serve man in his work, are born as human for their association with human and their last desire is to be like the master.

These are only a few of the cases we talked about. Each case presented for judgment is unique, as we all are, but there is a very fair and kind way our Father God judges to help us grow further in our spiritual progress till we are fully awakened to our reality and go back home with God from where we all started in Satjug. In Treta and Duapar, we distanced ourselves from God under the influence of rajgun and tumgun. Now, in kaljug, most of us are totally blind to our reality. It is in this period that God sent His messenger Guru Nanak to show us the way back to our reality through Naam which cleans up all our sins:

"Paap khandan Prabh Tero Naam." p-894

So Gurbani only teaches the way back through Naam; and to prepare for it we have to be truthful in thoughts, words and deeds which is called satgun and allows limited indulgence in rajgun and tumgun to control the five doots of Maya.

As mentioned in earlier cases, the only way which works back to spiritual progress is through the human body and acquiring wealth of Naam instead of focusing only on material wealth. This will, at least, ensure our rebirth in the human body. Once we become rich enough in the wealth of Naam God promises us, through Guru Ji, in which we will be blessed to reach home for bliss forever and will not have to go through this hell of rebirths and living through grief again.

Reincarnation is not a philosophical idea, but a part of a plan of God to get us back to where we came from. Our destiny is not an automatic act like the concept of Karmas in the Hindu faith, but is Lekh, the destiny written by our ever loving and forgiving Father God who cares for us in whichever form we are. He only tries to make us to learn through hard times and gives us happiness and good times to keep loving life and playing the roles He assigns to us in His Play on this Earth, which Gurbani calls Dharamsall- a school of spiritual learning.

God lovingly embraces whosoever comes to His sanctuary; this is the way of The Lord and Master:

"Jo saran aavay tis kanth laavay eh birad Swaamy sandaa." p-544

Even the ungrateful to Him are taken care of by God, O Nanak. He is forever the Forgiver:

'Akirtghnaa noon paalda Prabh Nanak sud bakhshand." p-47

LAAVAAN

The Four Laavaan, or four wedding hymns, was written by Guru Ram Das Ji describing, in a nutshell, the four developmental stages of spiritual awakening of the human soul bride in its efforts to unite with the Husband Lord. This spiritual marriage is performed in four laavaan, or rounds, with each leading to the next higher spiritual step to reach the fourth step when, finally, the spiritual marriage takes place for a permanent union.

In the first round, soul bride learns its mundane responsibilities and spiritual duties from Gurbani and cleanses itself of the sins of the past lives through truthful living and meditational remembrance on the Name of God. This brings inner peace and taste of sweet nectar from within.

In the second round, soul bride is blessed with a vision of Satguru from within. This eradicates the filth of ego, eliminates all fears and brings in the respectful fear and love for God in the mind who then starts singing His praises in the company of true saints. The mind now starts hearing Anhad Sabad, the unstuck divine melody from within.

In the third round, the mind, in love with the Lord, starts longing to meet Him and keeps singing His praises in the company of true saints who helps it to have His vision. The mind now dwells on the Lord- longing to be with Him.

In the fourth round, the mind becomes tranquil and united with the Lord, Who blesses it with divine nectar, which brings bliss to the mind. Now the mind enjoys the sweet nectar and hears the divine song all the time. In this blissful state, the soul bride has found its heart's desire, the Love of the Husband Lord, and keeps thanking the Lord who, Himself, arranged this union.

Here is the translation of the Four Laavan:

By God's Grace begins the first round of marriage
It is my duty to understand temporal duties of life   1
Then learn and practice on the teachings of Gurbani
This will make me renounce the sinful deeds in life   2
Grasp and act on the true spiritual duties as a human
Practice meditative remembrance on God's Name   3
Worship and adore the true and perfect Guru within
All sins caused by ill deeds will then be dispelled   4
By good fortune my mind has tasted the inner bliss
And God has blessed my mind with sweet nectar   5
Nanak proclaims that by end of the first round
Marriage ceremony has made a good beginning   6 I1I

By God's Grace begins second round of marriage
Lord has arranged for me to meet with True Guru   1
By His Grace my mind has lost all worldly fears
This has eradicated the filth of ego from my mind   2
With loving fear of Immaculate Lord in my heart
I am singing His praises and behold His presence   3
The True Lord is the Soul spread within me and is
Master of entire Universe pervading everywhere   4
Deep within and outside He is the only One Lord
Meeting His servants, the true saints I sing in joy   5
Nanak proclaims by the end of the second round
Unstruck melody of utterance of the Lord is heard.   6 I2I

By God's Grace begins third round of the marriage
I am filled with Love and longing to meet the Lord   1
Lord blessed me with company of True saints
With good fortune they helped me meet the Lord   2
I met the Immaculate Lord and sang His praises
Now my mind only thinks and talk about the Lord   3
It is my good fortune that I met with true saints
And I keep telling others how to meet with the Lord   4
My heart resounds with Divine Song of His Word
As destined now my mind only dwells on the Lord   5
Nanak proclaims that by the end of third round
My mind is constantly longing to be with the Lord.   6 I3I

Progressing to the fourth round of the marriage
Mind becomes tranquil and is united with the Lord   1
The devotee has met the Lord with intuitive ease
Who blessed my mind and body with divine nectar   2
God now likes me enjoying His gift of sweet nectar
In divine love I focus my mind day and night on Him   3
I have found my heart's desire, My Master and Lord
All congratulate me over gift of Naam from the Lord   4
My Lord and Master Himself has arranged this union
In bride's heart now blossoms the enshrined Naam   5
Servant Nanak proclaims in fourth round of marriage
I have found My True Love, Eternal Husband God.   6 I4I

Here is a message from Guru Ji about how in Kaljug, Naam is the only way for liberation from Maya. Since it is the last jug of this cycle of the Four Jugs, God is very kind to grant the gift of Naam to all His devotees to cross over Bhavjal Sagar by meditating on Gursabad to start the next cycle in Satjug. All others will perish, as Gurbani states, at another place:

"Naam rahio sadhu rahio Gur Gobind.
Kauh Nanak is jagat meh jin japio Gur mant."

GLORY TO TRUE NAAM

The perfect Lord has created
    a perfect universe in He permeates
In the world glory is to True Naam
    of God not the false ego one creates.   I1I

Imbibing truth of Guru's teachings
    'in our heart like Guru we become.
Enshrining Guru's Sabad within us
    Naam illumined our mind becomes.   IPauseI

Near end of Four Ages devotees
    are blessed with Naam's treasure.
Not celibacy self control pilgrimages
    in Kaljug God's glories sung measure.   I2I

Vedas and Puranas tell every age
    has its own way of emancipation.
Meditation on His Name achieves
    acceptance through mind's purification.   I3I

Nanak says through love for The True One
    mind's false ego dispelled forever
Utter listen to God's Name accept Him
    get a treasure of joyful peace ever.   I4I

Bilawal M-3 page 797

Here is a message from Guru Ji as to how God created the universe and that *everything is being controlled by Him. It is only in our ignorance, as self-willed manmukhs, that we think that we are in charge in this life. But, as things don't seem to go our, way we lament and suffer. The only way we can find relief is to accept Guru's teachings and take shelter in God's sanctuary and start accepting all that happens as His Will.*

GOD CONTROLLETH ALL

All happens in the world by Your Will
    if we could act on our own we would.
Beyond us to do anything on our own
    He maintains us here as He feels good.   I1I

O My Lord everything is in Your control
    powerless we receive all as Your gifts.   IPauseI

You gave this mind and body to us all
    to Your Will You make us act Your-way.
We act only as You command us to do
    as per our destiny You wrote Yourself.   I2I

Universe You created of components five
    let us see if anyone can a sixth make
To some You brief Your Will by true Guru
    others lament as self-willed You make.   I3I

Beyond me is to describe glories of God
    like a fool an idiot a lowly being am I.
O My Master forgive this servant Nanak
    to Your sanctuary come ignorant.   I4I

Raaga Soohe M-5 Page 736

Here is a message from Guru Ji describing our journey in life; telling us how we miss achieving the goal and suffer, and how, with our devotion to Him and His Grace, we make it to the bliss of His union through Naam.

LIFE'S JOURNEY

Visitors are we to this world born again because of ego.
Having lost our mind to Maya we commit countless sins.
Sunk in greed attachment and ego we remember not death.
Entire life goes dealing with family friends earning to live.
At the end of life sight of envoy of death scares we suffer.
Destiny of past cannot be erased without wealth of Naam.

Busy in worldly deeds we forget or sing not praises of God.
We wander in countless incarnations dying to be born again.
As animals birds stones trees and countless other forms.
Whatever we sow we reap it and face results of our deeds.
We lose jewel of human life and pleased is not God with us.
Lost and wandering thus we find not peace in our life at all.

Youth and its glory ends replaced by hardships of old age.
Our hands trembel head shakes and eyes see not well too.
Ready to depart without seeing God, meditated on Him not.
For those whom we cared for life obey us not but insult us.
Enshrined not love for the Infinite Perfect Lord in our heart.
Like a house made of paper this body gets perished quickly.

Nanak seeking the blessings of God fell at His Lotus Feet.
God helped me cross the terrible impassable world ocean.
Meditating amidst the holy God held me close and saved.
God accepted me blessing with Naam ignoring all my faults.
I got what I yearned for, Infinite Lord Treasure of all virtues.
Enriched by Him with His Divine Naam I am forever content.

Jaitsari Chant M- 5, p-705

Rabinder Singh Bhamra was born in 1940 and raised in the city of Amritsar in Punjab, India into an industrial family. He grew up with an interest in the fine arts and finished his college education at Khalsa College, Amritsar with a Bachelor of the Arts. Later, the author did his Honors Degree in Mechanical Engineering from IIT in Bombay, where he worked for six years as a Production and Quality Manager before migrating to Long Island, New York. The author has been living in New York since 1972 with his wife, Balwinder Kaur of Chandigarh. He worked as a Principal Engineer and Quality Manager in microelectronics and electronic components manufacturing with General Instruments Corp. Presently, he is working with County of Nassau as a Project Manager.

The author has been involved as a volunteer in the management of the Gurdwara Sikh Cultural Society since 1972 for 19 years until 1991, where he served as a General Secretary, Vice President and Trustee. He was one of the founding members of the Sikh Council of North America in 1978 and helped start the Sikh Day Parade on Baisakhi Day since 1988. He has also helped run the Sikh Studies Program at Columbia University for 10 years. As a community spokesperson, he presented the Sikh religion in interfaith meetings and conferences. He was working with JUS Punjabi T.V. till 2011, the first National

Punjabi T.V. Channel in the USA, as a Talk Show Host and Senior Correspondent. He is deeply involved in the spread of Gurmat through writing, lectures, katha, kirtan and TV presentations. The author is also an Honorary Chaplain with the Department of Police, County of Nassau, New York.

The author has also written a book in English poetry *GOD'S UNIVERSE AND MAN published in 2013.*

Printed in Dunstable, United Kingdom

63897599R00150